A History of Rest

A History of Rest

Alain Corbin

Translated by Helen Morrison

polity

Originally published in French as *Histoire du repos* © 2022 by Editions Plon, un Département de Place des Editeurs, Paris

This English translation © Polity Press, 2024

Polity Press
65 Bridge Street
Cambridge CB2 1UR, UK

Polity Press
111 River Street
Hoboken, NJ 07030, USA

ISBN-13: 978-1-5095-6152-0 – hardback
ISBN-13: 978-1-5095-6153-7 – paperback

A catalogue record for this book is available from the British Library.

Library of Congress Control Number: 2023951557

Typeset in 11 on 14 pt Sabon LT Pro
by Cheshire Typesetting Ltd, Cuddington, Cheshire
Printed and bound in Great Britain by TJ Books Ltd, Padstow, Cornwall

The publisher has used its best endeavours to ensure that the URLs for external websites referred to in this book are correct and active at the time of going to press. However, the publisher has no responsibility for the websites and can make no guarantee that a site will remain live or that the content is or will remain appropriate.

Every effort has been made to trace all copyright holders, but if any have been overlooked the publisher will be pleased to include any necessary credits in any subsequent reprint or edition.

For further information on Polity, visit our website:
politybooks.com

Contents

v

Contents

Acknowledgements

I would like to thank Fabrice d'Almeida, my editor, and Estelle Cerutti for her meticulous work on this book. Thanks also to Sylvie Le Dantec for her work on the manuscript and, as always, for her invaluable support.

Introduction

'Ah, if I'd only been capable of setting up my own business, I'd be comfortably stretched out on my back by now, taking things easy.' These words struck a chord in me. It was in 1977, and I was talking to a family friend. It was that idea of lying flat on your back, doing nothing and simply allowing your thoughts to wander. It reminded me of a novel called *Les Allongés*, written in the 1930s. Set in a sanatorium in northern France, the novel focused on the lives of bedridden patients each facing their illnesses in different ways. When I was at boarding school, the period between the two masses each Sunday, the only time for rest in the whole week, was supposed to be spent writing letters to our families ... All these little fragments came drifting back to me, reminding me of different ways of recuperating, now long forgotten.

Saying, or simply thinking 'I need to rest' is the expression of a desire, a feeling which we instinctively consider as the manifestation of a fundamental need, for both men and animals alike, which in a sense should belong outside the realm of history. Yet nothing could be further from the truth. Definitions and depictions of rest have varied continually over the course of centuries, often intertwined and overlapping, or even clashing with one another. Clearly, there is no common ground between the desire to one day obtain eternal rest and that of simply getting enough rest to keep 'burn-out' at bay.

As a child, I remember the frequently repeated phrase 'Don't disturb him, he's resting.' There was something solemn, almost sacrosanct, about such moments. Yet it was clear that the person concerned was not asleep. So, what exactly were they doing? Later, during my military service, our behaviour was ruled by three different commands: Attention!, Present arms!, At ease! These were repeated at each drill or parade and were associated with three clearly defined postures. 'At ease' was not an invitation to rest but simply implied a slight relaxation, as in sport when there is a pause between two exercises. An easing off, in other words. This book is not about those specific moments which mark a break between two activities. Rather, its intention is to examine the concept of rest as understood by our ancestors and to explore the intense experiences sometimes associated with it.

The book does not set out simply to bring together the results of the various studies on this subject, which are in any case relatively limited in number. Instead, by choosing to take an overview, our aim is to identify how depictions of rest and techniques of rest developed and multiplied over time by attempting to identify the high point of each of these and to chart their subsequent decline. This approach will highlight certain specific periods within the context of a history made up of multiple overlapping layers, of innovation and of inertia, and in the form of 'cultural flotsam and jetsam'.

Such was the importance of rest in times gone by that it permeated all forms of artistic creation. Paintings depicted scenes where individuals were shown withdrawing into themselves, all toil set aside. Literature also, as we shall see, portrays such moments. However, in this book, I wanted to focus in particular on sources taken from outside fiction in order to measure how social and human beliefs on this subject gradually took shape. As a result, except for some rare exceptions, I have avoided reference to novels.

The aim is therefore to embark on a journey leading from a time when rest was associated with salvation – in other words, with a state of eternal happiness – to the 'great century of rest', which, for the sake of simplicity, extended from the last third of the nineteenth century to the middle of the twentieth century. Following that, at varying intervals of time, came the new hedonistic image of the beaches with the triumph of rest in the sun symbolized by the fashion for sunbathing and tanning, the therapeutic rest advocated in sanatoriums, those new temples of rest, and the growing importance, in France, of the demand for paid holidays, seen as a period of rest intended to remedy the fatigue brought on by work.

In order to chart this journey, we must first retrace our steps to the very origins of rest and travel back to biblical times and that far-distant era when the Western world was created.

1

Sabbath and Heavenly Rest

For many ordinary people, the belief that, after the Creation, recounted in Genesis, God 'rested', was long seen as the foundation and the justification for resting on the seventh day. This belief refers to the sabbath rest of the Jews, as exhorted by various commands set down in Exodus, Leviticus and the Book of Numbers, though not in Genesis. This supposed rest taken by God, a belief shared by many ill-informed Christians, is not, according to the Church, that of a weary creator. Any such suggestion would be erroneous, since it would be at odds with the idea of God's perfection and his eternal nature and would reduce his status to the level of that of some of his creatures. In the eyes of Christian theologians, 'God's rest', celebrated on the first day of the week rather than on the seventh, is a 'creative pause' which initiates a 'fresh infusion of energy into creation', the beginning of a cycle. In short, rest, in this context, does not correspond to an absence of activity.[1]

Nevertheless, the instruction urging the faithful to rest on the seventh day is reiterated in the Bible. In Exodus,

Yahweh tells Moses: 'Speak to the sons of Israel and say, "You must keep my sabbaths carefully, because the sabbath is a *sign between myself and you* from generation to generation to show that it is I, Yahweh, who sanctify you. You must keep the sabbath, then; it is to be held sacred by you."'[2] This holy word which orders the observation of the sabbath makes it both a sign of the Alliance between God and his people and a sacred time which enables the faithful to be made holy. Yahweh's words to Moses do not stop there: 'The man who profanes it must be put to death; whoever does any work on that day shall be outlawed from his people.'[3] The severity of the sanctions is proof of the importance God attaches to the sabbath as a day of rest, particularly as he reiterates the call for the death penalty. 'For six days you shall labour and do all your work, but the seventh day is a sabbath for Yahweh your God.'[4] These verses define the meaning conferred on the seventh day in Jewish history and which Christians would take as their inspiration – albeit, it should be emphasized, in a modified form. This is not a day of rest purely in terms of relaxation but, above all, a day devoted to God, one which seals 'a lasting Covenant' and represents 'a Covenant in perpetuity'. Without exception, all Christian authorities emphasize that Sunday rest makes this a holy day.

In several of the following books, Yahweh repeats the command. So, for example, in Exodus, he specifies that on the seventh day you shall rest, 'even at ploughing time and harvest'.[5] Above all, he emphasizes once again that it will be *'a day of complete rest, consecrated to Yahweh'*.[6] What is important is not complete rest but the holy nature of that rest. 'You must not light a fire on the sabbath day in any of your homes.'[7]

God returns to the subject in Leviticus. He reiterates his commands and makes the sabbath the day 'for the sacred assembly',[8] thereby extending the significance of this seventh day.

The commentators of the Jerusalem School demonstrate what, in their opinion, constitutes the significance of the Christian Sunday: for the faithful, this coincides with the first day of the week (see chapter 10), when thanks are given to 'he who creates and re-creates the world . . ., he from whom came eternity'.[9] It is important to recognize the way in which Jewish and Christian biblical interpretations are intertwined.

Let us return to the Bible and, more precisely, to Leviticus. In this book we read about the creation in every seventh year of 'a sabbath for Yahweh', 'a year of rest for the land'. The creation of this period of time associates nature with the notion of rest.

> When you enter the land that I am giving you, the land is to keep a sabbath's rest for Yahweh. For six years you shall sow your field, for six years you shall prune your vine and gather its produce. But in the seventh year *the land is to have its rest*, a sabbath for Yahweh. You must not sow your field or prune your vine, or harvest your ungathered corn or gather grapes from your untrimmed vine. *It will be a year of rest for the land.*[10]

Furthermore, this 'sabbath of the land' will be accompanied every forty-nine years by a *year of jubilee*, preceding the fiftieth year, in the course of which the land will once again lie fallow. This period of rest for the earth deserves emphasis even though, according to the biblical commentators, it only applies specifically to the Holy Land and, consequently, Christians would not follow this command.

It was important to point out here the much reiterated biblical origin of the founding of the sabbath as commanded to Moses, a day Christians would transform into a Sunday and which would be a day of rest because it is one consecrated to God the creator.

Let us return to a reading of Genesis in order to turn our attention to another form of rest: that enjoyed by man, newly settled at the centre of the earthly paradise, the Garden of Eden. Indeed, it was the original sin, followed by the Fall and then the punishment of Adam and Eve, which resulted in man's mortality, the revolt amongst animals leading them to tear each other apart, and the obligation to rely on painful toil in order to survive. To make my point all the more clearly, let us turn to the most famous epic poem of the seventeenth century, Milton's *Paradise Lost*. The author gives a powerful account of the significance and the nature of heavenly rest and describes how man found himself deprived of it immediately after the Fall. His work represents an important contribution to the shaping of the imagery of rest and therefore deserves to be included in this study.

Milton depicts a specific form of heavenly fatigue and, at the same time, describes a type of rest unknown to man. During the day, Adam and Eve spend their time tending the garden: 'Under a tuft of shade that on a green / Stood whispering soft, by a fresh fountain.' Milton describes how:

> They sat them down; and, after no more toil
> Of their sweet gardening labour than sufficed

To recommend cool Zephyr, and make ease
More easy, wholesome thirst and appetite
More grateful . . .[11]

A subtle economy which defined a rest enhanced by a gentle fatigue – radically different from that which would, after the Fall, force them to seek rest. At the heart of the earthly paradise, rest was simply something to be desired, something which represented, in a sense, a 'gentle need', and which would be echoed in the rest taken by Adam and Eve in their 'bower' of leaves, inaccessible to all other creatures.

While the animals were playing: 'as they sat recline / On the soft downy bank damasked with flowers';[12] and

Handed they went, and, eased the putting-off
These troublesome disguises which we wear,
Straight side by side were laid; nor turned, I ween,
Adam from his fair spouse, nor Eve the rites
Mysterious of connubial love refused.

During all of that time they were alone– a fact which colours this rest with a particular emotion. Adam and Eve knew nothing at that time of other beings.

Night falls and, addressing himself to Eve, Adam draws links between their exquisite rest and that of nature: 'Fair consort, the hour / Of night, and all things now retired to rest / Mind us of like repose.'[13] For God had ensured that, for the man and the woman, work and rest, just like day and night, would alternate with each other. That said, the other creatures, with no tasks to accomplish, have less need for rest than man because, at the heart of the earthly paradise, the latter has a task assigned to him.

Milton continues with a hymn exalting conjugal love, associated with the nocturnal rest of the whole earth and experienced in a place safe from intrusion, except by the serpent. On the day following their punishment, when they were forced out of their earthly paradise, the first thing the unhappy couple did, according to Milton, was to 'choose their place of rest'.[14]

2

Eternal Rest, the Foundation Stone of This History

For almost two thousand years, the concept of eternal rest has been a major source of preoccupation and has fundamentally defined the notion of rest. Theologians, preachers, monks and ministers of all denominations have continued to emphasize that life on earth is of little significance and that what matters is salvation, or, in other words, the possibility of heavenly rest, in the company of the chosen and amongst the host of angels surrounding the Redeemer, God the Father and the Holy Spirit.

This explains the importance of the *ars moriendi* (the art of dying), of the prayers recited in funeral services during which the requiem was sung. The requiem constitutes the introit or opening for the mass for the dead, which, in consequence, is also known as the 'requiem mass'. This introit takes the form of a prayer for the rest of the soul of one or more deceased persons. The term *requiem* is, in Latin, the accusative singular of *requies*, which means 'rest'. The first words of the introit are: '*Requiem aeternam dona eis, Domine*', meaning:

'Eternal rest grant to them, Oh Lord.' Throughout the history of requiem masses, growing emphasis has been placed on the Last Judgement, the resurrection and the threat of everlasting damnation.

Preparing your salvation, or in other words escaping the clutches of the devil by avoiding sin and living in a constant state of fear inspired by that same demon, was an essential part of life. This is why natural disasters were interpreted as punishments sent by an angry God or as signs reminding people of the fundamental importance of salvation and the need to secure eternal rest.

But before such rest could be obtained there loomed the ultimate hurdle of the Last Judgement, long believed to be imminent. Near the recumbent effigies lying on their tombs, the façades of cathedrals and other churches evoked or depicted that terrible day when sinners would be cast into Gehenna and all its torments.

Roman and gothic sculptures loomed large in people's minds – though perhaps less, in truth, than is frequently claimed – instilling in them this horror of punishment and the fervent desire to attain the ranks of the chosen.

Before the nineteenth century – and I refer here to the major work on the subject by Philippe Ariès[1] as well as to other texts focusing on death in the eighteenth century – the deceased were not, as was later the case, buried in individual tombs. This privilege was reserved for certain elites and for members of the clergy. Nevertheless, with a view to facilitating rest while awaiting the Last Judgement, it was common practice to place the deceased in a supine position, like those effigies all of us recall seeing in places of worship.

It might be supposed that all of this belongs to a very distant history, to an era portrayed in the great trilogy of the historian Jean Delumeau, *La Peur en Occident – Sin and Fear: The Emergence of a Western Guild Culture* and *History of Eden in Myth and Tradition*. In reality, things are not quite so simple.

'Requiem masses', the ceremonies during which the requiem is sung, continue to be widely celebrated today, in spite of a certain decline in the practice. Many of the greatest musicians of our time have sought to add their own requiem to a long list of masterpieces, including those by Mozart, Berlioz, Verdi, Brahms and Fauré, whose *In Paradisum* magnificently portrays the sweetness of the eternal rest invoked for the deceased.

One of the great musical moments in the Christian history of this divine rest is to be found in the final minutes of the *St Matthew Passion* by Johann Sebastian Bach. After the corpse of Christ has been placed in the tomb and a heavy stone used to seal the entrance, the choir of the faithful repeats the chorus of 'Now the Lord is brought to rest!' And the account of the Passion ends with the reiteration, accompanied by the most sublime music, of the exhortation to 'rest softly, softly rest', a state which the faithful also wish for themselves when the time of their death arrives.

At the end of Handel's *Samson*, after the destruction of the temple and the death of the Philistines, the members of the cortège escorting the remains of the hero to his final home wish him 'rest eternal, sweet repose'. Once again, the association between rest and sweetness is reiterated. In this way, sacred music, in two of its most sublime examples, and away from the context of a requiem mass, expresses the hope that the deceased will find the sweetness of rest.

During the seventeenth century, Bossuet, in his sermon on death – one of the greatest texts in French literature – made a magnificent appeal for earthly life to be scorned in favour of the hope of eternal rest, a sentiment frequently echoed.

An analysis of the requiem hymn helps us to better understand the importance accorded to eternal rest and the need to regard this as the foundation for the historical variations of the multiplicity of images of rest – all of them inspired by the existence of short and often fragmented periods of time, far removed from the notion of eternity. One frequently evoked notion is that the 'rest of the dead' must not be disturbed, the worst version of this being the violation of a grave. Respecting the dead means avoiding any insult to their memory, and it is for this very reason that 'ashes must be left at rest' and that cemeteries are sometimes referred to as 'gardens of rest'.

3

Rest and Quietude

There can be no happiness without rest, and no rest without God.

Massillon, *Les Maximes et les pensées*, 1742

Pascal's portrayal of rest is extremely complex, and the fragmented nature of the texts does little to facilitate the analyst's task. In the first instance, according to the author of *Pensées*: 'Man finds nothing so intolerable as to be in a state of complete rest, without passions, without occupation, without diversion, without effort.'[1] Pascal explained this powerful assertion, stating that, in such circumstances, man 'faces his nullity, loneliness, inadequacy, dependence, helplessness, emptiness'.[2]

He specifies the various torments experienced by the individual 'in a state of complete rest': 'there wells up from the depths of his soul boredom, gloom, depression, chagrin, resentment, despair'.[3] Boredom is 'naturally rooted in our hearts', where it can 'poison our whole mind'.[4] The reader is reminded of the threat of *acedia* in medieval times[5] and cannot fail to be struck by the detailed list of the multiple emotions provoked by boredom. The paradox is that 'the man who loves only himself hates nothing more than being alone with himself'.[6]

Threatened by boredom, the consequence of complete rest, man constantly seeks to avoid this state by seeking diversion – in other words, movement, 'activity', 'agitation', turmoil, noise, gambling, all of which turn his thoughts away from his unhappy condition.

Whatever his state, the absence of 'diversion' makes man unhappy. The same is true of solitude. In short, he needs to get out into the 'hustle and bustle' which will 'divert him and stop him thinking about himself'. Without diversion, for man, 'there is no joy, with diversion there is no sadness'.[7]

Yet, Pascal insists, rest, though rejected, is paradoxically desired – sincerely and from the depths of the soul. A secret instinct drives man to rest, even though he does not truly know what it is. Pascal, for his part, observes: 'the sole cause of man's unhappiness is that he does not know how to *stay quietly* in his room'.[8]

A secret instinct drives men to seek distraction, but there is 'another secret instinct, left over from the greatness of our original nature, telling them that the only true happiness lies in rest and not in excitement. These two contrary instincts give rise to a confused plan buried out of sight in the depths of their soul which leads them to seek rest by way of activity.'[9] Yet, at a more profound level, they also seek rest in God. Indeed, in the conclusion of his *Pensées*, in a section devoted to rest, Pascal states that man 'must seek God'.[10]

In this seventeenth century, another factor emerges, and we shall now focus our attention on what constitutes

a fundamental element for anyone seeking to understand the exact meaning of what is referred to as 'rest
in God'. This is the notion of *quietude*, a concept which
at the time was the subject of fierce debates, including,
notably, the argument over *quietism*, which divided
theologians, bishops, ministers and pious individuals
at the end of that same century. During this period, the
notion of quietude lay at the very heart of our subject.
It profoundly coloured the secular notion of rest in
God. The Latin word *quies* means rest or quiet, and the
concept of quietude bears no relation to any notion of
fatigue. Indeed, it would be a serious anachronism to
think in such terms.

Let us pass rapidly over the genealogy of the
notion, except to point out that its origins were rooted
in the range of emotions experienced and described
by mystics from the preceding century. Teresa of Avila
considered that quietude was a great gift from God,
granted during the second stage of the ascent of the soul
to God.

During this stage, the person at prayer does not yet
reach the state of ecstasy, this 'delight the soul experiences', which will be attained subsequently. In the
course of this second stage the spark, granted by God,
is ignited. This represents the most precious of his gifts:
quietude. 'All the soul needs to do during these times of
quietude is be still and make no noise', even avoiding
expressions of gratitude towards God. In this state 'the
will' becomes one with 'rest'; phrases and speeches and
the 'the noisy intellect' fall silent. So, in these moments
of quietude, urges Teresa, we should 'put all learning
aside and *simply rest in the stillness*'. In this second
state, the worshipper places themselves entirely in the

presence of God, who wants 'to strip us of our reason and render us utterly foolish'.[11]

In the following century, François de Sales drew inspiration from Teresa of Avila but reflected at even greater length on the notion of quietude. His *Introduction to the Devout Life*, in which he explores the subject, enjoyed enormous success and became a source of inspiration to many young girls and women. François de Sales defined the state of rest that he called quietude, describing in detail how it could be achieved and the different levels on which it could be experienced. He provided advice on ways of prolonging this state which was all too easily lost. In order to explain his thinking more clearly, he turned his attention to evangelical texts.

This is how he defined quietude: the Sulamite bride[12] experienced a state of mind in which she was 'content' and 'at rest'. Yet, in the course of her prayer, 'this rest reaches such a point that the soul and all its powers are as though asleep, the will alone possessing any motion, and it merely accepts the satisfaction which the Presence of the Beloved imparts' – and all of that 'unconsciously'.[13]

The soul who in this '*exquisite repose*' enjoys this delicate sensation and 'thus hushed in its God would not exchange that rest for the greatest of earthly treasures'. So, Mary Magdalen, seated at the feet of Jesus,[14] listened to the holy word: 'There she sat perfectly still, not speaking or weeping, not even praying.' She is simply listening. Jesus assured her that she 'has chosen that better part, which shall not be taken away from her', and François de Sales emphasizes that this meant: '*Resting peacefully and in calmness* in the Presence of Jesus'.[15]

He then goes on to explain how this 'blessed repose' can be attained. Like the little child suckling at the breast, the soul 'hushed in rest before God' 'almost unconsciously ... sucks in the sweetness of that Presence',[16] without any fear. . . . Why would it not wish to remain at rest? asks François de Sales. In this state, it abandons itself to the pleasure of a presence while 'every faculty of [the] soul is hushed in a grateful repose'.[17]

In order to preserve that inner peace, we must avoid behaving like those who, 'instead of surrendering their will to the sweetness of the Divine Presence, . . . employ their minds in weighty feelings'.[18] 'The soul, then, to which God gives holy, loving quietude in prayer should abstain as far as may be, *from inspecting self or that rest*, which is in danger of being lost by overmuch contemplation'.[19]

Another instruction suggested that, if the soul cannot prevent itself from being distracted by the surroundings, attempts should be made to at least ensure 'the will remains at peace'. Most importantly, it should not be constantly striving 'to recall the other wandering faculties' such as the imagination, for in that case 'it would lose its own peace'.[20]

The subtlety of the paths of prayer, the interweaving of tranquillity and sweetness, the ability to no longer listen to oneself and, above all, the successful attainment of absolute rest for the soul merit inclusion in a comprehensive history of past times. The modern neglect of the notion of inner peace or quietude – but not of its opposite, in the form of anxiety or disquiet – must be regarded as a flawed historical approach.

Alongside Fénelon and François de Sales, the second half of the seventeenth century saw the emergence of the powerful personality of Bossuet. It will come as no surprise that this staunch enemy of quietism took a very different view of rest. Except in some rare references, he refrains from glorifying it. In his sermon on death, Bossuet robustly reveals his thinking, an approach which corresponds to that held by the Church. Rest is above all eternal rest. Death places man in a waiting state, at rest, and the individual who leaves behind his 'former abode' – the body – is destined to be renewed again. God, Bossuet assures us, 'gives us rooms wherein we may *await in peace* the complete reconstruction of our former abode'.[21]

Bossuet was impressed by the grandeur of monastic rule, in particular as established by St Benedict and by Bernard of Clairvaux, both of whom he regarded with great admiration, addressing a number of panegyrics to them. Reading these, however, there is scarcely any reference to rest as we would understand it in this twenty-first century. Periods of prayer and of meditation sufficed to restore the strength needed to carry out tasks. As for the faithful, Bossuet considered, in his second panegyric on St Benedict, that the 'paths of perfection' did not include rest, since the path trodden by Christians meant that they must remain 'always alert and eager'. This is, he assures us, the intention of the saint. Indeed, the belief that we have reached our goal means 'we relax our efforts; slumber overtakes us, we perish'. The Christian is constantly threatened by the 'drowsiness of the soul' against which he must constantly battle. 'There is', Bossuet insists, 'a languid portion of our being which is always ready to fall asleep, always weary, always oppressed, seeking only to be allowed *to take some repose.*'

The flesh, that languid and slumberous part of man, invites him to take a little rest, saying softly: 'See, all is calm and peaceful; the passions are conquered, all hurricanes and tempests have quieted down, the sky is serene; the sea is smooth, the vessel glides gently on, needing no guidance; . . . surely you may *allow yourself a little repose*?' And the spirit . . . reassured, too, by the smiling stillness of the waters . . . lets go the helm, suffers the ship to take her own course, and falls asleep; a great storm springs up, the vessel is submerged.[22]

These powerful marine and maritime metaphors, which are a subtle reminder that the sea voyage symbolizes the life of the Christian on his journey towards salvation, are typical examples of the references to the cosmic world that are so central to Bossuet's writing. Furthermore, in his opinion, the Benedictine rule, 'a learned and mysterious abridgement of the whole Gospel teaching',[23] highlights the danger that the soul might be subjugated by rest.

This tension between, on the one hand, the exaltation of quietude, or rest in God, and, on the other, the temptation of rest with the inherent risk of shipwreck is a good illustration of the complexity of the very notion of rest in the Catholic theology of the seventeenth century. We will find it again in the Age of Enlightenment when, associated with the secularization of the notion of rest, and in the face of the acclamation of quietude, there came a rising tide of anxiety, so well analysed by Jean Deprun in his book on the philosophy of anxiety in eighteenth-century France.[24]

4

Retreat and Retirement in the Seventeenthand Eighteenth Centuries, or The Art of Being Able 'to Forge' a Tranquil Rest for Yourself

One form of rest much debated in the seventeenth and eighteenth centuries is that associated with 'retreat' and 'retirement'. Largely the domain of men and, to a much lesser extent, of women, this is the time when those who have lived should 'enjoy what they still have', as La Rochefoucauld would put it. At the end of the sixteenth century, Montaigne, who returns to the subject on several occasions, begins by identifying the moment when it is appropriate to seek rest in retirement. It is a time when an individual observes: 'We have lived quite long enough for others; let us live at least this tail-end of life for ourselves. Let us bring our thoughts and reflections back to ourselves and to our own well-being.' 'Our powers are failing: let us draw them in and keep them within ourselves.'[1]

This is, all too often, a difficult decision. 'Preparing securely for our own withdrawal is no light matter'; 'let us pack up our bags and take leave of our company in good time'.[2] Some temperaments are 'more suited than others to these maxims about retirement'. It is, in particular, more difficult for 'those busy active minds which welcome everything with open arms, which take on everything, get carried away about everything'.[3]

Montaigne considers at length the decision we should make to withdraw in favour of our children. A father 'who is brought low by age and illness, whose weakness and ill-health deprive him', should simply 'want to get stripped and lie down'.[4] Therefore, his advice to a nobleman who was a widower and 'very old but still with some sap in him' was to leave his house to his son and withdraw 'to a neighbouring estate of his where *nobody would trouble his rest* ... He later took my advice and liked it.'[5]

What is most important – and this applies to the wisest individuals – is *to forge a rest for yourself*. Montaigne outlines a series of tactics for those seeking to attain this goal.

Retreat – or retirement – is first of all a process of relinquishment. Montaigne lists all the things that must be left behind: 'A man who withdraws ... should have taken leave of toil and travail ... and should flee from all kinds of passion which impede the tranquillity of his body and soul, and choose the way best suited to his humour.'[6] 'Ambition is the humour most contrary to seclusion. Glory and tranquillity cannot dwell in the same lodgings.'[7] For a stoical individual, the best course is to devote this part of your life 'to obscurity'. 'A man who withdraws pained and disappointed with the common life must rule his life by a diet of reason, ordering it and arranging it with argument and forethought.'[8] He must flee anything that threatens his tranquillity.

At the moment of retirement, every individual must find rest within themselves. Montaigne urges us to 'make our happiness depend on ourselves', to 'bring out thoughts and reflections back to ourselves', retreat into our inner selves, live 'for ourselves', 'marry nothing but ourselves'.[9] That said, however: 'we should retain just enough occupations and pursuits to keep ourselves fit and to protect ourselves from the unpleasantness which comes in the train of that other extreme; slack and inert idleness.[10] So, he concluded, we should read only 'pleasurable, easy books' or 'those which console me and counsel me how to control my life and death'.[11] In other words, far better to train and sharpen your appetite to what pleasures still remain and to concentrate on what age has not yet snatched from us.

Any occupation that must therefore be preferred 'should be neither toilsome nor painful . . . It depends on each man's individual taste.'[12] Montaigne admits that he utterly detests the task of managing his estates and advises anyone who envisages 'an ample and thriving retreat' to leave to his servants 'the degrading and abject care' of his estates.[13] Montaigne dismisses any obstacles which might make men avoid rest because of fears that it will lead them to succumb to boredom.

One century later, La Rochefoucauld carefully lists

the reasons that naturally cause old people to withdraw from dealing with the world. The changes in their temperament and appearance, and the weakening of their bodies, imperceptibly lead them, like most other animals, to draw back from the company of their own kind. Pride, which is inseparable from self-love, then becomes their substitute for reason. It can no longer be flattered by various things that flatter other people's pride . . . but also because they have seen the death of many friends . . . they no longer have much share even of glory. . . . Every day takes away some part of themselves; they now have too little life to enjoy what they still have, and even less to gain what they still desire. They see before them only discomforts, afflictions, and debasement; everything is familiar, and nothing can have the charm of novelty for them.[14]

In La Rochefoucauld's thinking, such pessimism is scarcely tempered by any more positive thoughts. For those who have retired, 'their taste disillusioned with futile desires', there remains only things which are forced to suit their wishes, which they approach or distance themselves from according to their whim, making everything centre on them. 'Their taste . . . turns then to silent, insensible objects – building, agriculture, economics, study' – in all of which 'they are in control of their plans and activities'.[15]

But the argument goes deeper. La Rochefoucauld refers to Lucretius, addressing himself to someone who has retired: 'Why, you fool, do you not retire from the feast of life like a satisfied guest and with equanimity resign yourself to *undisturbed rest*?'[16] It goes without saying that, in such a period, rest is not a response to fatigue but a detachment, the absence of care, the desire to flee all forms of agitation. Rest, in this sense, is a relaxation which allows the mind to be renewed and enables the individual to attain wisdom and serenity, without forgetting that idleness 'is like a blissful state of the soul, which comforts it for all its losses, and which acts as a substitute for all good things'.[17]

Referring to the need for rest, and in agreement with Montaigne, La Rochefoucauld considers that, 'When you cannot find peace within yourself, it is useless to look for it elsewhere.'[18] Yet he evokes the fear of finding yourself, which, in his view, is different and more serious than simple boredom.

A great many seventeenth- and eighteenth-century moralists turned their attention to the subject of rest. Their comments more often than not reinforce previous observations on the subject. According to Madame de Sablé: 'The possession of many goods does not bring the repose of not desiring them';[19] and, in the words of Étienne-François de Vernage, 'man's rest relies on the calm state of his passions and on the removal of needless worries and cares. It is in vain that he seeks for it elsewhere.'[20]

The perceptiveness of La Bruyère's observations marks them out from amongst this cohort. He proclaims *'the best of all good things ... is repose, retirement* [note the link], *and a place you can call your own'*.[21] 'Life is short and tedious, and is wholly spent in wishing; we trust to find rest and enjoyment at some future time, often at an age when our best blessings, youth and health, have already left us.'[22] La Bruyère emphasizes the value of rest as an object of desire; in response to the question posed by fools as to how he amuses himself, his answer is: 'in enjoying health, rest and freedom'.[23]

Dufresny observes how, in his entourage, *rest is an object of desire*, particularly amongst courtiers. One of them, aged seventy-five, confided to him: 'I have worked a lot, and I have worked solely in order to have the means to live at rest; I sincerely hope to be able to rest in a few years' time.' Disillusioned and ironic, Dufresny adds: 'I would venture to say that those of this nature work themselves to death, in order to rest for what remains of their lives.'[24]

The same sentiment is mockingly expressed by Diderot a century later. Describing travellers embarked on a boat which is in the process of sinking, a scene depicted by Joseph Vernet in a painting of which Diderot was the delighted owner, he imagines the thoughts of one of them, raging because he had promised himself considerable profits at the end of the crossing: 'Alas! he had reckoned on a prosperous voyage; this was to be his last, and then he would retire to enjoy ease and tranquillity. A hundred times during the voyage he had calculated what his capital would be, and how he would invest it, and now all his hopes are disappointed.'[25] Man is himself either in a state of tumult or at rest, writes Diderot, in his *Essai sur la peinture*, 'and the moment of tumult and the moment of rest have this in common, that in them each person shows themselves as they are'.[26]

On the cusp between the eighteenth and nineteenth centuries, Joseph Joubert, in his *Carnets*, returned on many occasions to the subjects of old age and of rest. He urged: 'Rest for the good! Peace for the tranquil!'[27] The first of these two states is, in his view, essential, since 'being deprived of rest means much to the soul. Rest is of no small matter to it. It represents a state where the soul is uniquely free to follow its own movement without outside impulses'.[28] far from disturbance: 'Disillusionment in old age is a major discovery.'[29]

Returning to an idea expressed by the moralists who had preceded him, Joubert insists that 'working in order to have nothing to do is how human life is spent. Movement leads to rest, rest preserves the self, nourishes it from within.'[30] This exaltation of rest goes hand in hand with that of old age, which brings with it wisdom. 'Neighbour of eternity, [it] is a kind of priesthood.'[31]

Interlude: Charles V

Let us mark a short pause here and turn our attention to the most famous example of retirement in the sixteenth century, notably that of Charles V, which began on 18 September 1555. In this case, the image of rest is permeated with a number of other intentions concerning the exact nature of this retirement, which entails a mixture of renunciation, detachment, the art of dying well and a profound desire for rest. Charles V was fifty-five years old at the time. It is worth remembering that, in the mid-sixteenth century, the two other major monarchs, François I and Henri VIII, had died at the age of fifty-two and fifty-five respectively.

A number of factors lay behind the retirement of Charles V. First of all, the temptation to retire or stand down was a tradition amongst Spanish monarchs and was very much part of Spanish Christianity. Charles V had in fact nurtured plans to step aside for some considerable time and had voiced his wishes on the subject as early as 1535. Moreover, his health was deteriorating. He had suffered from gout since the age of thirty, and by the age of forty-seven he appeared to observers as an old man, one hand paralysed, his leg often bent beneath him. He also suffered from diabetes.

Religion played a very important role in his life. He practised fasting, mortification and sometimes flagellation. He liked to withdraw to a monastery and spend time in prayer.

Charles V had been preparing his plans for retirement for a considerable time and had chosen where he would spend his final days. Amongst the three traditions with which he had ancestral links – Burgundian, Austrian and Spanish – he opted for the latter and decided to spend his retirement near the Spanish monastery of Yuste, situated in Estremadura and belonging to the order of St Jerome. It was, however, in Brussels, on 25 October 1555, that he solemnly abdicated from the long list of his responsibilities and powers,[1] handing them over to his son Philip II, then king consort of England, through marriage to Queen Mary Tudor.

The journey to the monastery of Yuste was complicated on account of atrocious weather and delays in the construction of his humble place of retreat. In fact, Charles V did not become a monk, as has sometimes been claimed, but settled in the immediate vicinity of the monastery of Yuste, in a modest but comfortably furnished house decorated with eight paintings by Titian and various familiar objects.

During the few months of his stay, Charles V enjoyed direct access to the monastery and could take part in services from his apartment. Was he able therefore, during that time, to enjoy a period of rest, far from the agitation of the world? This was undoubtedly the case to some extent, but the answer to this question is far from simple. His retirement was not a total one, and a series of letters, reports and requests kept him in touch with world events, ranging from the victory of Saint-Quentin to the loss of Calais suffered by the English, which he heartily condemned. But more than any potential threats to the various borders, it was the advance of Lutheranism, into the very heart of Spain, that most strongly provoked his anger.

During his time in Yuste, he made preparations for a holy death. The former emperor, it is worth reiterating, regularly followed the services of the monastery in the form of masses, vespers and compline. Each day, he listened to one or more sermons and heard readings from the Bible. Before going to bed, he recited a long prayer. His confessor, who remained constantly at his side, was an important presence within his modest residence.

Charles V had at his disposal a small library which allowed him to access many sacred texts but also some works of history, particularly those relating to the Burgundian tradition. He could walk regularly in the little garden adjacent to his lodgings.

On 21 September 1558, it was neither gout nor diabetes which finally caused his death but instead the malaria which was at that time rife in northern Estremadura. His end was an uplifting one. He called on his assistants to help him die and uttered the name of Jesus as he drew his last breath at two in the morning.

Do these few pages merit their place in a book dedicated to rest? The answer may perhaps be unclear, but it is nevertheless possible that Charles V, having experienced so much turmoil in his life, found at Yuste, in the period following his abdication, a sense of detachment which, for him, very much resembled rest.

5

Disgrace, an Opportunity for Rest

Let us now consider the subtle status of rest imposed as a result of disgrace. During the seventeenth and eighteenth centuries, and in particular in what was then the kingdom of France, disgrace – which meant being deprived of the king's presence – took on a key significance within court society. For members of the aristocracy, disgrace meant being forbidden to appear at court and being forced to abandon the tumult of Parisian life and instead withdraw to their country estates. Some years ago, I examined in detail the notion of this provincial territory which had inherited some of its elements from an association with disgrace.[1]

Within court society, the French provinces were considered a form of hell, an internal exile which condemned the victim to lethargy and to a symbolic death. Being away from the excitement and bustle of court life meant being condemned to the torments of boredom. Disgrace was comparable with simply rusting or mouldering away. The fear of being forgotten at court and in the city further exacerbated the pain of being distanced from those places.

Yet, if we turn to Pascal, disgrace was an opportunity for rest – for, from that moment onwards, for those who are in disgrace, 'no one stops them thinking about themselves'.[2] Exile could become a kind of desert in which the inner self could begin to blossom. Viewed from this perspective, rest could be seen as compensation for the pain of disgrace, with enforced idleness encouraging reflection and allowing the individual concerned to discover new ways of savouring life, far from the agitation and tumult of the court – though not, however, without some lingering regrets.

A reading of many of the personal accounts of this experience reveals the subtle nature of this form of rest. In fact, during the period of disgrace, letter writing was stimulated by the distance now enforced and writing of a personal nature enriched by the absence of frenzied activity, all of which, in a subtle sense, harks back to epistolary practice from a much earlier era. Disgrace could, moreover, provide opportunities to indulge in walks or rides, or for social encounters which, albeit on a smaller scale, reflected those of the court, or it could stimulate an interest in the restoration of one or several chateaux. All these factors, in a sense, echoed the *otium cum dignitate* of ancient Rome, tinged with stoic resignation.

As an example of this, the extensive correspondence exchanged between Bussy-Rabutin[3] and the Marquise de Sévigné allows a glimpse of the complex psychological intertwining which was so characteristic of the former: a combination of the pain of disgrace, the appeal of '*otium cum dignitate*' and, beyond that, renunciation, resignation and the pleasure of a compensatory rest. It is this latter that makes his case of relevance here.

Bussy-Rabutin, cousin of the Marquise de Sévigné and a valiant military figure, fell into disgrace under Louis XIV, in 1659, as a consequence of having revealed information about the king's activities in his writings. He was banished from both the court and the city and forced to retreat to his chateaux in Burgundy. Let us attempt to summarize his prolific body of writing. Bussy-Rabutin considered his disgrace as a form of exile but acknowledged that it allowed him to experience life in a way different to the frantic activity of life at court and the hustle and bustle of the town. While awaiting his 'return to grace', he occupied his time in the upkeep and improvement of his chateaux, making various 'adjustments', receiving a great many visitors and going to Dijon, where a reduced version of the court was in operation. He savoured the pleasures of this 'little regency'. He was touched by the expressions of loyalty which still came to him from Versailles, and he consoled himself by observing that, all things considered, he was better treated than some other disgraced individuals. On that subject, he cites the companions of Nicolas Fouquet, the extravagant superintendent of royal finances incarcerated in the prison of Pignerol.

What is particularly relevant to our subject here is that Bussy-Rabutin combines the notion of resignation with that of rest. On 12 August 1680, he confided to the marquise:

> The length of my disgrace has rendered me indifferent to anything concerning my fortune, and I think only of living well and of seeking pleasure. . . Since God willed it so, I am

as fond of the gentle and peaceful life that I have led for the last few years as I am of a more eventful one. I made sufficient noise in the past.[4]

This withdrawal from the activity of court life, which would have delighted Pascal, filled the marquise with joy, and sixteen days later she sent this reply to Bussy-Rabutin: 'I am overjoyed, . . . that you are at last able to rest in your chateau and to hear that you are putting your time to good use in philosophizing and moralizing for one cannot think as clearly as you do without being well fortified against the cruel obstinacies of fortune.'[5] And Bussy-Rabutin replied, on 4 September: 'As for time for reflection, we devote ourselves to it as much as great idleness allows.'[6] In short, he showed that he had, at that stage, managed to put aside all thoughts of the bustle of court life and of the torments of disgrace and, having resigned himself to his lot, was savouring a genuine period of rest.

During a short stay in Paris, undertaken with the permission of the king, he admitted to Madame de Sévigné, on 25 June 1680 – a particularly interesting year because of the various changes in Bussy-Rabutin's circumstances: 'For the evils that Providence imposed on me by ruining my fortune, I long hesitated to believe that this was for my good, as my spiritual directors insisted; . . . I refer not only to my good in the other world, but also for my rest in this one.'[7]

6

Rest in the Midst of Confinement

Can confinement or imprisonment lead to enforced rest? Nothing could be less certain. It is important to emphasize here that our notion of seclusion and the relationship it might have with rest does not include the case of monks who chose to remain secluded in their monasteries, the better to fully devote themselves to prayer and to secure their salvation, far away from the bustle of the world. Such individuals often found themselves constrained to work for much of the time, though without ever losing sight of the fact that they were awaiting eternal rest. Those incarcerated in prison, on the other hand, very rarely perceive their situation as an opportunity for rest. From Silvio Pellico to Prince Louis-Napoléon, shut away in the Fortress of Ham,[1] some have written accounts of their experience and have shared their political thinking. Prison played an important role in the life and work of the Marquis de Sade, though without any direct reference being made to the importance of the notion of rest.

It was an altogether different matter for more simple forms of confinement, whether voluntary or not, temporary or more enduring, resulting from the vagaries of nature or from decisions relating to health or legal matters, or even in some cases simply occurring as a matter of individual choice. Goncharov based his novel *Oblomov* on a fictional case which was both extreme and unforgettable.[2] Let us turn our attention to some real and well-documented cases of confinement. Montaigne claims to have encountered someone who, of his own accord, shut himself away for many years until his death. According to the author of *The Essays*, this individual suffered from melancholy. The reader could reasonably suppose that, for this recluse, it was simply a matter of turning his back on the bustle of the world and choosing to enjoy his own company in peace. As well as agitation and commotion, inopportune intrusions also represented another threat to rest. Consequently, the seventeenth century is marked by a loathing of the people referred to as 'les fâcheux'.[3]

The person Montaigne was referring to was Jean d'Estissac, a dean of Saint-Hilaire-de-Poitiers. There is no indication, in this case, of a decision provoked by the desire for a hermit-like existence, or, in other words, for a solitary life devoted entirely to God.

> When I went into his room, he had not set foot outside it for twenty-two years; yet could still move about freely and easily, apart from a rheumatic flux discharging into his stomach. He would let scarcely anyone in to see him even once a week; he always stayed shut up in that room all by himself except for a valet who brought him his food once a day and who merely went in and out. His only occupa-

tion was to walk about reading a book . . ., obstinately determined as he was to die in those conditions – as soon afterwards he did [in 1576].[4]

Confinement can be the result of a natural event. Just such an occurrence provided the inspiration for *The Heptameron*, by Marguerite de Navarre, a masterpiece of French literature. Although this is a fictional depiction of rest in circumstances associated with confinement, it seemed appropriate to include it in this book in so far as it follows 'an ancient tradition of fictional characters who find themselves in dangerous or unusual situations',[5] cut off from the miseries and troubles of the world.

In this fictional case, the confinement is a collective one and involves an interruption to normal activities and a period of rest furnished with many distractions. A small group of men and women of noble descent are travelling back from the spa town of Cauterets, where they have taken a cure, and find themselves cut off when the River Gave bursts its banks. Following the deaths of some of their number, the survivors take refuge in a monastery where, over the course of the following days, they are made welcome by 'the good lady Oisille'. The flooding gets worse and, from that point on, the group seek out some entertainment in order to 'alleviate the boredom' which threatens to make them fall sick with sorrow.

Hircan, a member of the group, observes that the guests of Lady Oisille, who, unlike her, 'have not yet become so mortified in the flesh', need some amusement to fill the time between dinner and vespers, 'some pastime, which, while not being prejudicial to the soul, will be agreeable to the body', and which would ensure that all of them 'shall spend a very pleasant day'. In short, Hircan proposes that they transform their period of confinement into a time of pleasure and of rest for the soul.

Parlamente, one of their number, comes up with an idea, inspired by Italian literature, whereby

> we could go each afternoon between midday and four o'clock to the lovely meadow that borders the Gave de Pau, where the leaves on the trees are so thick that the hot sun cannot penetrate the shade and the cool beneath. There we can sit and rest, and each of us will tell a story that he has either witnessed himself or which he has heard from somebody worthy of belief.

In that way, 'at the end of our ten days we will have completed the whole hundred'.[6]

The following day, all those faced with the threat of boredom as a result of being deprived of their accustomed pastimes find themselves sitting on the grass, 'so green and soft that there was no need for carpets or cushions'. A situation which, in this time of confinement, combined religious practice – in the form of rest for the soul – and joyous rest for the body in the midst of grassy meadows. And the stories begin . . .

In French literature, the most famous text to emerge from confinement in the strictest sense must still be Xavier de Maistre's *Voyage Around My Room*.[7] In reality, this young soldier, held under arrest in a room for a period of forty-two days, is spared that real seclusion which would have been the lot of a condemned man locked away in prison. Xavier de Maistre takes advantage of this imposed isolation to experience a type of rest which we shall now examine in more detail.

Reading the text in which he describes the pleasures of confinement, it is impossible not to think of Pascal's writings on the benefits of being at rest in a room. At the time de Maistre was writing, in the late eighteenth century, the doctrine of temperaments linking personality traits to the circulation of humours in the body was already on the wane, but he would certainly have been classified amongst those subject to a lymphatic temperament – a category of individuals with a penchant for rest. In her introduction to the French edition, Florence Lotterie[8] refers to his 'smiling indolence'. Xavier de Maistre, who moreover came from a solidly classical background, relished the delights of *la flânerie* – that is to say, a mode of strolling somewhat akin to a state of rest.

After a peaceful youth, de Maistre's life in the Russian armies was interspersed by periods of rest. Reading his biography, a clear tension emerges between his being constantly on the move and being confined in a single place. Like many of those writing later, in the nineteenth century, de Maistre was evidently savouring 'the new manner of travel' and found himself succumbing to the temptation of the closed space as somewhere in which 'to withdraw and hide from the world'.[9]

In this context, the bedroom must be seen as the ultimate place of rest. As such, and especially at this time, when the attraction of a private life was increasingly felt, it deserves a place at the very heart of our subject. It acts as a defensive wall, a refuge, a place where pleasures can be enjoyed in solitude and where a particular form of rest can be experienced. It is not simply a matter here of a bed, of sleep, or even of the hypnagogic sensations which precede it and which should not be confused with periods of rest.

The rest we are referring to here derives from the pleasure of being alone in your bedroom. This place is in a harmonious relationship with the subject's consciousness and therefore inspires a specific type of rest dependent on the presence of familiar and unchanging objects, often associated with family history or, at the very least, linked to a personal past. These references to family and personal history speak to the individual confined in his or her room and prevent any feelings of personal detachment.

Let us now briefly turn our attention to the dressing gown. At the time in question, this garment was endowed with a particular significance amongst the various objects which symbolized and even embodied rest. The pain Diderot felt on the loss of his old dressing gown is evidence of a long-standing association with a particular item of clothing, transforming it into a quintessential symbol of rest.

> Why not have kept it? It suited me and I just suited it. It followed the lines of my body without cramping me. I looked well and picturesque . . . My old friend, too, was always at hand to serve me in any emergency . . .
>
> Under its shelter, I feared no mishaps, neither those of my valet, nor my own, neither sparks from the fire nor splashes of water. I was complete master of my old dressing-gown . . .
>
> Where is the venerable, humble, and comfortable piece of chintz?[10]

At the very end of the nineteenth century, after Hugo and, even more, Baudelaire had both described similar experiences, the Belgian poet Georges Rodenbach skilfully analysed the discourse centred on the bedroom and its objects. It is in the bedroom that the sensation of rest is experienced with a particular force, at certain times, and during certain rituals. On this subject, Xavier de Maistre highlighted the sensation experienced on first waking up and the particular flavour of breakfast. All of these intensify the pleasures of rest, experienced and enjoyed in a place safe from agitation and from the horrors and miseries of the world.

Of course, such feelings are also associated with the convenience and comfort not only of the place itself but also of the objects designed with rest in mind, which will be examined in more detail in the next chapter.

Xavier de Maistre describes in detail certain gestures which indicate a state of rest and enhance the sensations involved. Let us read what he has to say on the subject: 'I must admit that I love to savor those sweet moments, and I always prolong as much as possible the pleasures of meditating in the sweet warmth of my bed.' Elsewhere he stresses the pleasure 'of feeling myself doze', an experience he describes as 'a most exquisite enjoyment unknown to many! One is awake enough to perceive that one is not entirely so and to reckon vaguely that the time for business and worry is still in the day's hourglass.'[11]

Another quality of rest, and an even more powerful one, is that, according to Xavier de Maistre, it intensifies friendship – curiously he does not refer to love. Writing about a friend who has recently died, he laments that the death occurred 'just at the moment when our bonds were growing stronger in an atmosphere of rest and tranquillity'.[12]

In conclusion, on the subject of the link between the bedroom and the notion of rest, let us turn once more to de Maistre, who, in emerging from 'that enchanted realm containing all the wealth and riches of the world', observes 'how my ideas have changed, and my feelings too'.[13]

7

The Quest for Comfort: New Approaches to Rest in the Eighteenth and Nineteenth Centuries

Confinement can be associated with a desire for comfort and practicality, as La Bruyère demonstrated when he sketched the portrait of Hermippus, who 'looks ... everywhere' for 'his little contrivances', which are indispensable to the quality of his rest. Although this is of course fiction, let us bend the rules a little here and briefly overturn our decision not to use it as a means of observing practice.

Hermippus 'must see his bed made' and doubts if anyone 'is so skilful or fortunate to make it in such a way that he can sleep as he likes'. Anxious about the quality of his rest, he controls his gestures, his movements, seeking to perform all tasks 'in a short time and without much difficulty'. Initially 'compelled to take ten steps to go from his bed to his lavatory; he has now so contrived his room as to reduce these ten to nine, so he saves a good many steps during the whole course of his life!'[1]

La Bruyère describes the search for these practical 'little contrivances'. Some time later, during the eighteenth century, measures like these acquired even greater significance. The quest for practical ways of enhancing the quality of rest became more intense as new and more refined forms of relaxation gradually emerged. This period, wrote Georges Vigarello in his admirable text on the subject,[2] saw the emergence of a more sensitive individual, someone increasingly focused on their personal feelings, and this led to a more intense scrutiny of the immediate environment with a view to improving the quality of rest and, even more importantly, to refining both the sensations involved and the accessories which enabled people to enjoy the experience.

The quest for comfort involved seeking out previously unknown ways of adapting the external space to the newly discovered internal one and enhancing the way people used their space, allowing them to experience certain specific pleasures by providing opportunities to rest in different physical positions.

'Attitudes are changing', wrote Vigarello, 'rest is undergoing transformation'; new furniture was being designed to suit a gradual move towards a 'more relaxed physical posture' and even a 'conspicuous nonchalance'.[3] Previously, the vertical seat, by nature of its solid structure, forced the sitter to keep their back straight and their legs in a vertical position. Now, though, along came various types of easy chair, designed to provide increased comfort and enjoyment. This marked the advent of furniture designed specifically for rest.

Georges Vigarello describes in detail the initial stages of this process, which, through the play of interactions, brought in its wake new physical demands, new 'prototypes for rest'. First of all came backrests designed to fit in seats. It was in this period that the actress

Mademoiselle Clairon adopted a semi-reclined posture, 'nonchalantly stretched out on a chaise longue, her arms crossed, her eyes closed and motionless'.[4]

In the same period, a new item of furniture, also known as a 'duchess', allowed the user to preserve a seated position while extending their legs thanks to a kind of 'shelf' which formed an extension to the chair with its slightly sloping back. This piece of furniture was called a 'chaise longue' because it had eight feet which enabled it to be carried. So, when a person was comfortably installed on it, rest took on a different aspect for the spectator confronted with this highly conspicuous demonstration of physical relaxation.

The rocking chair, of English origin, marked a new phase in the growing trend for an increasingly ostentatious display of rest positions. The rocking movement and the opportunity it provided to gaze up at the sky while resting proved to be a source of new and delightful sensations. In this case, the rocking motion, reminiscent of the experience of a very young child in its cradle, was an innovative source of comfort. Over the next decades, the rocking chair underwent further adjustments, enabling further improvements to be made to the resting position. The fabrication of the rounded chairback, then the advent of upholstery, the increasing variety of different shapes available, the design of the cushions, meant, writes Georges Vigarello, that gradually the seat 'deliberately sagged under the weight of the user'.[5] The firm seat was replaced by an accumulation of soft layers, eventually leading to the design of the kangaroo sofa, which first appeared in the United States. This reflected the physical shape of the body, 'the sinking down of the pelvis, arched neck, bent knees'.[6]

Then came the era of the adjustable seat, adapted to suit a full range of rest positions. It was no longer the armchair but the individual who controlled the degree of physical relaxation and the chosen rest position. At the end of the nineteenth century, the deckchair made its appearance on the decks of ocean liners, an enduring symbol of an item of furniture designed with rest in mind, with an adaptability destined to remain popular for a long time, since in the twentieth century, as we know, it rapidly became omnipresent on beaches and terraces. And let us not forget that it spawned an image in people's mind whereby the soul and the body could abandon themselves to a languid state, in an atmosphere conducive to sensuality.

This brief history of the quest for comfort and of the objects that have played a part in shaping modes of rest saw the concept of relaxation replacing the more ancient concept of quietude, associated with rest in God. This new approach was a far cry from the preceding one, typified by its own iconic furniture item in the form of the prie-Dieu, or prayer desk, still very much present in bourgeois households during the nineteenth and twentieth centuries.

Another focus for research in the context of changing attitudes to rest would be the history of the positions and postures associated with it . . . everyone has their personal memories of yoga, for example. This is, however, a history which lies beyond the scope of our project. To make this clear, let me cite something Xavier de Maistre observes in *A Journey Around My Room*. During his incarceration, he invented positions associated with rest and tranquillity. So, for example, he would settle into his armchair, 'having leaned backwards to the point where the two front legs were raised a couple of inches from the floor'; then, by balancing from left to right, he managed to move the chair, and himself, forward. More adventurous is a position which he describes as a combination of rest and expectation: 'I slid to the edge of my armchair, and setting both feet on the mantelpiece, I patiently awaited my meal. What an exquisite position.'[7]

8

Prelude:
Rest in the Midst of Nature

Aside from the contributions of the philosophers already cited, certain classical references, though not necessarily directly acknowledged, have continued to exert a significant influence on the depictions of rest which are the subject of this book. So, for example, the modes of relaxation described by Virgil in his *Eclogues* (also called *Bucolics*) and, to a lesser extent, in his *Georgics*, have continued to occupy a place in many people's minds since the Renaissance, an enduring tradition evidenced by Paul Valéry's translation of the *Bucolics*, accompanied by *Variations*, his long preface to this masterpiece.

We will leave aside the arcadian tradition, which, with its two opposing faces, restful and violent, sits uncomfortably in a history of rest. As for the idyll and the influence of Theocritus, although he may indeed be regarded as the inventor of the bucolic genre, the portrayals of rest in his work are generally less varied and less intense than in Virgil's.

Virgil depicts rest as a desirable and exhilarating experience to be enjoyed in pleasant surroundings (*locus amoenus*), in an atmosphere suffused with *mollitia*, a delightful mellowness and a sense of refinement 'bordering on the effeminate'.[1] We know this represents an imaginary place where dreams are played out. Yet it must still be considered relevant here given the extent to which this *locus amoenus* has continued to influence the Western imagination. It is a delightful place where rest can be enjoyed as a prelude to sleep. The sensations experienced by the characters have certainly exercised a powerful influence on the dreams of Western readers and in particular on those writers who, like Ronsard, have depicted scenes of people resting on grassy slopes, under trees and near a fountain.

In order to demonstrate this more clearly, let us cite some short extracts from the exchanges between some of Virgil's characters. In the Third Ecologue, Palaemon, the shepherd, urges:

Sing both, for on the soft grass we are set,
And field and tree are with new verdure clad.

And Menalcas, speaking to Mopsus, in the Fifth Bucolic:

Singer divine, such is thy song to me
As sleep on grassy lawns to weary heads.

In the Seventh Bucolic, Meliboeus urges Daphnis: 'If thou hast leisure, rest beneath the shade.' And Corydon, also present, cries:

O moss-pillowed fountains, grass softer than sleep,
Green arbutus netting the shimmering shade,
Lo! Summer is here: bid him scorch not the sheep

Damon, we read in the Eighth Bucolic, describes Daphnis:

> Weary and lorn on couches of green sedge
> Beside a stream she sinks.[2]

The myth of Tempe, explored in the *Georgics*, would long be considered the epitome of an exquisite place where happiness and tranquillity reign, and the 'fortunate old man' from Tarentum, the model of happiness, if not of rest, is often cited by those sixteenth-century writers who, as we have seen, describe or yearn for a place of retreat. The *otium*, or cultivated leisure of ancient Rome, practised by the elite, was not, strictly speaking, a period of rest. The work of elected officials still went on, acting as a backdrop to the preoccupations of individuals who had taken refuge far from the Senate, following the example of Pliny the Younger, who chose to live in his Tuscan villa. Nevertheless, some amongst this group expressed the desire for a period of leisure devoted to rest.

For example, in Martial's *Epigrams*, we can read a declaration, made by a friend of the author, expressing a yearning to live for himself, a sentiment which might be regarded as the expression of a longing for genuine rest:

> If we could arrange our leisure as we wished and free up both our time for ready living, we'd know nothing of the entrance halls and mansions of powerful men, of frowning lawsuits and the gloomy Forum, of haughty ancestor-masks. Instead, going out for a drive, some plays, some little books, the Campus, the portico, a bit of shade, the Virgo, the baths. That's where we'd be, that's what we'd work at. As it is now, neither of us lives for his own benefit.[3]

Prelude: Rest in the Midst of Nature

It would be very dangerous to reduce to just a handful of individuals all those who have shared their experience of rest in the midst of nature. Their numbers are so great that a vast body of works edited by those specializing in the literary history of attitudes to nature is devoted to them. We will not cite them here. Instead let us consider this subject from a more distanced perspective, and in a condensed form, in order to illustrate, in broad brushstrokes, the evolution of the emotions and sensations associated with rest experienced in the midst of nature.

In order to do this, we have chosen to focus on two individual experiences, one taking place at the time of the Renaissance and depicted by Ronsard, and the second that of Jean-Jacques Rousseau in the eighteenth century, coinciding with the birth of what is referred to as the 'sensitive soul'. In Rousseau's case, the experiences described were much more widely shared and more subtle than they would have been at the time in which Ronsard was writing.

In the case of Ronsard, this choice poses another problem. Can it be valid to seek out portrayals of rest, experienced in the midst of nature, during and around the early modern period with a view to determining to what extent they represent a new approach? I have already announced my intention not to refer to examples taken from novels given the tactics to which these often resort in order to create an illusion of reality. Put briefly, such fiction does not constitute proof of emotions felt within the social circles depicted, in contrast to the various forms of personal writing such as diaries, autobiographies or correspondence. . . .[4] What then of poetic texts, since I have chosen here to look at rest as depicted in Ronsard's work?[5]

Clearly, the very act of writing a poem is, initially at least, a literary activity, and it might therefore be considered that this would disqualify the contents from inclusion in anything pertaining to a history of behaviour. Yet the situation is not so simple. Certainly, when Ronsard describes the experiences of resting in the verdant setting of the forest of Gastine, nothing proves that this is not simply the product of his imagination. Perhaps, in reality, he never experienced this kind of rest. We must nevertheless acknowledge that it seems highly plausible that such experiences did indeed take place. In this book, my intention is primarily to identify and examine new depictions of rest, along with the circumstances and, in some cases, references which explain them. Whether Ronsard himself reclined on the grass or not in no way invalidates the range of emotions associated with rest which he describes in his work. Indeed, the innovative nature of such experiences, and the scale on which they were read, justifies their place in this history of rest.

There is one element in Ronsard's work which might be considered a surprising attitude for a Christian. He broods at length about the decrepitude of old age – a stage which for him represents the antechamber of death:

> The old man cannot walk,
> Nor hear, nor see, nor chew
> He is a smoked statue
> Beside the hearth.[6]

Old people, burdened with their many years, are: 'crippled, maimed, full of catarrh, impotent'; and later, speaking of himself, Ronsard wrote:

I am nothing but bones, I seem but a skeleton,
Emaciated, feeble, without muscles, without flesh,
Such that the stroke of death has knocked without leave.
I dare not look at my arms for I should tremble with fear.[7]

This portrait is a far cry from Montaigne's depiction of old age or from that portrayed by the moralists we have already cited. For Ronsard, death is not the gateway to rest in God, with the exception of his epitaph for the Abbess of Poissy: 'And in peaceful and drowsy rest / May sleep her ashes and her bones. . . .'[8] Ronsard refers only rarely to salvation, and I was able to find just two references to quietude, including the well-known line '*dormez en doux repos*' (sleep in sweet rest).[9]

Most significantly, hope is largely absent from his poetic work, and the corpse is essentially an inert mass which has lost all sensation:

But the body, food for worms,
Stripped of veins and nerves,
Is no more than a sepulchral shadow.
It has no more mind nor reason
. . . but sleeps
Buried deep in a tomb.
It can no longer speak, nor hear nor see.[10]

And in his elegy for Philippe Desportes:

God alone is eternal, of elementary man
There remains after death neither vein nor artery:
What is worse, he can no longer feel, no longer reason,
Emaciated inhabitant of a lonely old tomb.[11]

Ronsard devotes a considerable number of magnificent pages to the theme of death, though without any mention of prayers, of *ars moriendi* or, as already mentioned, of eternal rest in God. It is clear that he draws inspiration more freely from the ancient pastoral tradition or from the work of Petrarch than he does from theologians. Nevertheless, he attaches significant importance to the grave and the oft-reiterated desire that his own grave and those of the women he has loved should be covered in greenery, an image which links together the notion of *post-mortem* rest and the fascination exerted by nature in the springtime, with its powerful symbolism.

There is also another underlying element in that Ronsard frequently reiterates his hatred of sleep, 'brother of death'. According to him, sleep is the very antithesis of rest; hence his horror of the bed, which he refers to as a hellish theatre of boredom, except of course when he finds himself lying there tormented by the pangs of love.

> I seek to find an excuse not to go to bed,
>
> I read some book or other, or pretend to be writing, . . .
> Or alone I walk about and walk about some more,
> Trying to distract with a memory the boredom that
>   devours me . . .
>
> Bed is hell to me, as though in it,
> Someone had thrown glass or sharp thistles:
> Now on one side, now on the other.
> I turn, weeping, and cannot there remain.[12]

Yet, during his lifetime, Ronsard was someone who delighted in opportunities to rest in a pastoral environment: the legacy, it is worth repeating, of a classical sensibility which was more bucolic than Arcadian – in spite of the success of Sannazaro's poem entitled *Arcadia*. In the course of a series of poems he described how he rested and sometimes fell asleep on the grass and on 'the thick moss', both in the forest of Gastine and, more specifically, close to the Bellerie fountain.

> Listen to me, lively Fountain,
> Where I have so often drunk
> Lying flat upon your bank
> Idle in the fresh breeze.

Or in 'A la Fontaine Bellerie': 'In summer I sleep or rest on your grassy bank, / where, concealed beneath your green willows, I write . . .'.[13] And, for example, with reference to the Gastine forest: 'Lying under your green shade, / Gastine, I sing to you.'[14] And, in Ode XVII, entitled 'To His Mistress':

> To drink on the soft grass
> I want to stretch out under a bay tree
> And wish that Love with a little gust . . .
> Would lift her thin dress to her thigh . . .[15]

Ronsard seeks rest in these places for a number of reasons: first of all, out of a desire to ease the weariness caused by writing poetry. He craves rest after too much writing, when 'his spirit urged him to do it no longer', 'bringing rest to my capricious spirit'. . .[16]

Most importantly, Ronsard appreciates the bright freshness of the grass and the breeze. Close to the fountain, the sound of the stream brings him 'rest for the spirit'. At times, his writing clearly refers to the Virgilian *locus amoenus* – for example, his references to Corydon, or the comparison with Tityrus.[17] In addition, he describes with a particular intensity the sensual pleasure of reclining on the grass, sometimes the backdrop for erotic frolics or the memory of them.

Having dealt with the subject elsewhere, I am not referring here to novels published a little later, in particular *L'Astrée* and *Le Grand Cyrus*,[18] both of which feature a number of scenes depicting characters reclining at ease on the grass. Although Ronsard's writing is largely poetic in intention rather than written in the form of a personal account, it nevertheless reflects an experience which, in all probability, is not entirely fiction, like the novels I refer to.

Two centuries later, reading Rousseau, in works such as *Julie, or the New Heloise, The Confessions* and, especially, *Reveries of a Solitary Walker*, the experience of rest enjoyed in the midst of nature takes on a heightened intensity, partly at least because of the greater variety of types of rest described.

A great many studies have concentrated on Rousseau's travels and on the places where he chose to spend time surrounded by nature. At the risk of perhaps being over-reductive, I have chosen to focus only on references to rest. Amongst the most important works on this subject, notably *The Confessions* and *Reveries of a Solitary Walker*,[19] rest does not simply describe a period of idleness, even though Rousseau sometimes refers to moments of *farniente*. In his writing, rest involves fleeing the frenzy of social activity and the 'importunate crowd' in order to find tranquillity. According to him, rest is experienced in a place of refuge or shelter; and, in his case, that means being surrounded by nature – once he had successfully 'detached myself from social passions'. 'What do we enjoy in such a situation? Nothing external to ourselves, nothing if not ourselves and our own existence. As long as this state lasts, we are sufficient unto ourselves, like God.'[20]

Prelude: Rest in the Midst of Nature

Rest, according to Rousseau, is a state which is part of a complex strategy:

> *What is needed is neither absolute rest not too much agitation*, but a uniform and moderated movement having neither jolts nor lapses . . . If the movement [of the boat] is irregular or too strong, one is awakened. By reminding us of the surrounding objects, it destroys the charm of the reverie . . .[21]

Here then is the key word: what follows is a description of the particular quality that this state of reverie confers on rest:

> Movement which does not come from outside then occurs inside us. One rests less, it is true, but also more pleasurably, when light and sweet ideas only skim the surface of the soul, so to speak, without disturbing its depths. . . . This kind of reverie can be enjoyed wherever we can be quiet.[22]

Rest associated with reverie is an internal state, enjoyed in a place where there is nothing to remind us of the existence of others.

Alone in the middle of the lake, he writes: 'stretching myself out full-length in the boat, my eyes turned to heaven, I let myself slowly drift back and forth with the water, sometimes for several hours'.[23] It is worth emphasizing the posture adopted to facilitate this state of reverie and to evoke a specific form of rest. Simply being there, on the shore of the lake, was enough, he adds, 'to make me feel my existence with pleasure and without taking the trouble to think'.[24]

To my mind, this represents the very essence of what constitutes the nature of the state of rest combined with the freedom of the reverie: 'a simple and permanent state which has nothing intense in itself but whose duration increases its charm to the point that I finally find supreme felicity in it'.[25] In this sense, reverie links back to quietude, in a century where, as Jean Duprun demonstrates, the individual often felt threatened by multiple sources of anxiety.

The experience Rousseau enjoyed and recorded, an experience coloured by the sensations of nature, and in particular those produced by the motion of the lake, brought with it a discipline of its own, which involved emptying the mind or, in other words, refusing to dwell on 'sorrowful objects'. Giving free rein to the gentle sensations provoked by elements from the surrounding natural environment, particularly in the most delightful and secluded locations, inevitably led to tempting thoughts of a much dreamed of retirement, of finding yourself sequestered in a place where you could end your days in tranquillity.

In the account of his 'Seventh Walk', Rousseau writes: 'the meadows, the waters, the woods, the solitude, above all, *the peace and rest* to be found in the midst of all that are incessantly retraced in my memory by my imagination make me forget men's persecutions, their hatred, scorn, insults. . .'. Transported 'to peaceful habitats among simple and good people . . .', this combination of peace and rest 'recalls me to my youth and innocent pleasures; it makes me enjoy them anew. . .'. [26] This reference to the importance of past memories seems to represent a new element in the history of representations of rest.

In one of his *Propos*, dated 18 January 1909, the philosopher Alain[27] analyses Rousseau's experience of resting in his boat. He identifies an element which is central to this book. According to the philosopher, there is no single form of rest which remains constant throughout an entire life. On the lake, Rousseau savoured a type of rest which corresponded to a particular stage in his life, marked by his desire to escape from the agitation of society. He would probably not have had this type of experience with the same degree of intensity at any other period in his life, particularly for example during his youth, a period in which he often took long walks.

In inviting us to explore the differences between the desire for rest and the experience of rest at different times throughout our lifetime, Alain is exploring an avenue which goes much further than the simple allusion I have made to the specific nature of rest sought and experienced during old age and retirement. An examination of the typology identified by Alain would allow a deeper exploration of the history of rest, but this would necessitate a considerable undertaking which would lie beyond the scope of our intention in this book.

Might it be that this joyous time of happiness and rest, experienced by Jean-Jacques during his two-month stay on the banks of Lake Bienne, and the opportunities it brought for sublime contemplation, corresponded to a possible exacerbation of a sensitivity to weather conditions, a condition common at the end of the Age of Enlightenment? This does not appear to be the case. Rousseau, to whom we owe the famous expression, so often quoted, referring to the 'barometer' of the soul, does not appear to have been susceptible to this and showed no sign of being permanently alert to any associations between variations in the weather and fluctuations of personal mood. This concordance, on a day-to-day basis, as indicated and experienced later by a certain Maine de Biran – and this is but one example – seems not to feature in the range of emotions described by Jean-Jacques.

Yet, at the very end of the Age of Enlightenment, the growing interest in the influence of the weather on the inner self did exert a certain influence on representations of rest, or at least of retirement. Remaining aloof from the turmoil of the Revolution, in the manner of Joseph Joubert, was a form of retirement, a desire to distance yourself from the tumultuous events that were unfolding and to take refuge instead in the contemplation of the sky.

> Far from this place of horror, from this abyss of evils,
> I will go, I will fly to the bosom of rest.[28]

This was the very antithesis of comments made by Saint-Just, cited in the 1905 edition of *Larousse*, and urging total commitment: 'For Revolutionists there is no rest but in the tomb.'[29]

Let us digress for a moment in order to pursue this thread. In France, the nineteenth century was an era marked by bloodshed, unrest, turmoil, rebellion, uprisings and revolutions. Little attention has been paid to the intensification of the longing for rest, frequently experienced by people of all social classes, as a consequence of these violent events. The importance placed on the notion of 'political rest' in dictionaries, and notably the 1861 edition of Bescherelle, published in the middle of the century in question, is significant in this context, since it draws attention to a sentiment very often neglected by historians, who tend instead to emphasize the turmoil and agitation of the time.

Let us look at some definitions from this dictionary. The author of the entry immediately emphasizes the importance of the very notion of 'public rest' at this time, when people value 'a rest from politics'; he refers to the need felt during periods of unrest to 'restore public rest', 'which must not, in any circumstances, be disturbed'. The forms of turmoil cited are, first of all, 'disturbance of the public rest'. On the other hand, when the unrest calms down, the general view is that 'the people will enjoy a profound rest'. The ideal time is one 'when the country is in a state of complete, absolute rest'. In line with my comments on certain contemporaries of the Revolution, the author of the entry writes that, in troubled times, 'rest is a haven'. *He emphasizes, in such circumstances, the pleasure of being 'deep in the bosom of rest'.*

Let us return to the theme of nature. At the very time, let us remember, when Rousseau was spending long hours dreaming and resting in his boat drifting peacefully on Lake Bienne, England was gripped by a new and rapidly growing vogue for the beach. This raises the question as to whether the seaside holiday should be included in a history of rest. Would it be fair to claim that this new passion for the beach was, at that time, having a dramatic effect on the very fabric of rest?

I do not think this is the case. Let us, however, consider certain arguments which could possibly be advanced in support of this suggestion. Ever since the enormous success of Robert Burton's seventeenth-century study of melancholy, a link between rest and treatment had gradually gained acceptance. Undoubtedly the popularity of seaside holidays may have been in part associated with the possibility of treating patients with nervous conditions often associated with melancholy or, more broadly, those subject to depression, as well as invalids suffering from a general decline in their state of health.

Rest by the seashore was, for these limited categories, considered to be therapeutic. It is all too easy to forget that the English penchant for holidays on the shores of the Mediterranean, and the enforced rest that came with such stays, preceded the invention of the beach and continued for many years, echoing the splendour of Brighton and the English Channel resorts.

From the dawn of the eighteenth century, English doctors had begun advising patients to spend time – though not to bathe – in the towns of southern France. The popularity of this type of seaside vacation was so widespread that, in England, the word 'montpellier' entered everyday language to denote a restful place to stay. During a visit to Nice, the great writer Tobias Smollett kept a diary which became an important source for the history of the seaside holiday, with its many associations with rest.

Already, in the preceding century, Burton recommended the choice of Brighton as a cure for melancholy and advised people to stay somewhere where it was possible to enjoy the proximity of the sea. It is certainly the case that during the second half of the eighteenth century, when taking a cure in a seaside resort was becoming increasingly popular, in England many invalids, or those suffering from melancholy, were opting to stay in restful seaside locations – though rarely in fashionable resorts.

In two earlier books I referred to the case of Baronet Torrington,[30] author of a magnificent diary written on the Isle of Man, where he chose to spend a period of eleven months in 1789. The baronet had not gone there in order to bathe or to immerse himself in the waves. Every day, after a careful study of the weather – for he had a highly developed sensitivity to weather conditions – he went out for walks, seeking places where the gentlest sea breezes would allow him to experience the most subtle and, as he believed, most healthy sensations. When he left the island, he advised invalids in need of rest to visit the Isle of Man and, with the help of a certain number of reasonable but not excessive physical exercises, regain their strength. Reading his diary allows us to discover the various strategies for rest which were consistent with those recommended in vacation resorts as described above. These were, however, very different to the health cures in certain coastal locations, to which we must now turn our attention.

From the mid-nineteenth century onwards, as we shall see, rest was perceived as the antithesis of ordinary work and involved taking a break from activity in order to remedy fatigue. Before this time, rest had been associated with a retreat from any form of turmoil and agitation into a state of quietude and self-reflection, an experience which brought deeper self-understanding and the potential to experience a range of agreeable sensations. In the eighteenth century, when a great many people took up residence in the countryside, might it be that they were primarily in search of rest?

At that time, the countryside exerted a powerful attraction for the aristocracy of Georgian England. For whole seasons at a time, far from the king and the court – and motivated furthermore by the need to save money – these aristocrats retreated to their country houses and estates and spent their time hunting, riding and walking, sometimes collecting plant specimens in the lanes and fields and, when evening came, entertaining guests. All of which, in a sense, suggests a reworking of the classical *otium*, motivated by the desire for a dignified lifestyle rather than simply by the need for a restful existence.

Might there therefore be a case for including in the history of rest the seawater cure practised at that time in resorts all around the coast and based on the treatment devised in the 1750s by Doctor Richard Russell? I think not. We must be careful not to allow ourselves to be misled by a gradual shift in perception, slowly taking hold from the 1860s onwards, which saw the beach change from a place of medical treatment to a space devoted to hedonistic enjoyment.

Before that time, nothing about these places suggested the type of rest described earlier in this book or the sort Rousseau was able to experience. Brighton, the ultimate flagship resort, was, in social terms, an imitation of Bath. A master of ceremonies presided over the casino and supervised fashionable social relationships. The resort, like others dotted around the coast, had been created by leading members of the aristocracy, notably the brothers of King George III. The arrival of members of this social class would be announced in the newspapers, particularly during the 'season'. Essentially, the social frenzy that Rousseau was fleeing on the other side of the Channel was being re-created in these fashionable resorts in a mirror image of that associated with life at court. On this subject, an account of a sea-bathing session enjoyed by George III in Weymouth in 1789 is highly telling. It took the form of a ceremony attended by a troupe of nymphettes. In France, much later, at the time of the Restoration and under the influence of the duchess of Berry, the court would relocate to Dieppe during the summer season.

These places, however, were also associated with a considerable number of activities which were the very antithesis of rest in a state of quietude. The treatment advocated by Dr Russell and his followers drew its inspiration from natural theology. It relied on the power and the sheer immensity of the sea, regarded as the ultimate cure. Consequently, there was little opportunity for rest. Destined in particular as a cure for female ailments and for glandular problems, the treatment Russell had devised was based on the effects of immersion in cold water and the tensing of the muscles and was a far cry from any notion of quietude and relaxation. The water into which male, and especially female, bathers were plunged had to be at a temperature of 12 or 13 degrees. For his wealthier patients, he recommended that, prior to bathing, a bucket of sea water should be poured over their heads. The female bather was transported in a horse-drawn carriage and then plunged, head first, into deep water, with the help of a certified bathing assistant. This practice was known as sea bathing and relied on the effects of sudden exposure to cold water and the resulting muscular tension – the very antithesis of rest. As for men, they were required to swim in a vigorous and athletic manner – undoubtedly an extremely tiring activity.

Although doctors generally prescribed a short afternoon walk in dunes exposed to the wind, evenings could be spent in the casino. To sum up, it would only be with considerable reservation that such therapeutic practices could be included in a history of rest.

Everything would change, and we will return to this subsequently, when the sun ceased to be regarded as an object of abhorrence, when bathing costumes became simpler and, above all, when time spent on the beach began to be regarded as a source of hedonistic pleasure. And that would happen only at the very end of the nineteenth century and, more particularly, in the course of the twentieth century.

More closely resembling rest, and inspired by the vogue for hill walking popularized by Rousseau, was the fresh-air cure, advocated at the end of the Age of Enlightenment by Swiss doctors and in particular by the Swiss physician Théodore Tronchin. With a certain amount of caution, in view of the inherent risk of fatigue involved, such walks with their views of dramatic landscapes and exposure to the wind and fresh air could be considered as a premonitory form of rest (see below), in spite of the fact that, very often, the hectic social life of this group of people continued unabated.

9

A Rest for the Land

A 'rest for the land', as we have seen, was ordained by God every seven years and on the sabbath in jubilee years. In other words, the land, like man, had to rest. This might be seen as a reference to the fact that the land needed periods of rest – what is referred to in Western culture as letting the land lie fallow – but this is not our subject here. Instead, we are interested in a different form of rest, one that is linked to the rhythm of the seasons. We are already aware that this was a focus of interest to the painters and writers of the seventeenth and, in particular, the eighteenth century.

The rhythm of agricultural work has been the subject of endless descriptions and dictates since ancient times. But let us turn our attention, more specifically, to the way rest was depicted in the context of those who worked on the land.

In the temperate countries of the Western world at least, the winter season corresponded to a scaling down of activities, though certainly not to a period of rest as we would understand it. Indeed, it is clear that rest took a very specific form in the context I am referring to here. In this respect, considerable caution needs to be exercised if we are to avoid the temptation of anachronism. Is it good practice for historians to seek out examples of rest, as we understand it, when it is by no means certain that, for these people, the term would have had the meaning we automatically impute to it?

Let us give this matter careful thought. In the rural environment, the term 'rest' had a double sense. Firstly, it meant the eternal rest we have already discussed here: the requiems chanted during funeral ceremonies, visits to the graves of ancestors, and the attention paid to sermons on the *ars moriendi* were all opportunities to consolidate this depiction of rest, no doubt even more intensely in protestant countries, where family prayer was a well-established practice. Secondly, the interruption to activity on a Sunday, referred to as 'Sunday rest', took on an additional meaning, also with religious overtones.

Beyond this, a certain caution is called for. Rest, for the people in question, had no specific value as such. Zeal, dedication to work, a contempt for idleness, a loathing of the lazy, of 'idlers', of 'good-for-nothings', were indicators of esteem both for oneself and for others and inevitably led to rest being to some extent stigmatized. Those moments when work was briefly interrupted – pauses on a journey, conversations in a lane, at the edge of a plot of land, on a bench outside the home, social gatherings and a variety of evening events – all constituted a sphere of social interaction, of local community and of entertainments and celebrations. What we are now inclined to consider as rest was undoubtedly neither perceived nor referred to in such terms.

In everyday life, a woman's first duty – apart from the recital of prayers – was 'to keep herself busy', to ensure she could always find something to do, even if it was no more than an endless succession of small tasks. Women who, very often, were responsible for keeping the inside of the house as clean and as tidy as possible, doing the washing and spreading the laundry out to dry, feeding the poultry in the chicken-run, carrying out all sorts of small jobs in the garden, often feeding the cattle and, especially, looking after young children and preparing meals, could calibrate the difficulty of these various tasks and, when they needed to 'relax' – and not to rest – they could turn their attention to less onerous tasks such as mending clothes, knitting, etc. In their old age, women would devote themselves to these minor tasks and to looking after children until the very end of their lives.

As for men, once they reached old age, they often made it a point of honour to make themselves useful in small ways and to keep the fire going so that the inside of the house was kept warm and food could be cooked. Let us end this catalogue here, since it serves no other purpose than to draw attention to the risk, incurred by the historian, in trying to identify, in this context, examples of what we collectively regard as rest. I would suggest that it was only much later, as a result of slow changes leading gradually to mechanization and motorization, that our conception of rest finally took hold amongst those who worked the land.

Implicitly, in these rural circles, the system of tasks took into account the level of weariness of those who undertook the most arduous work in the fields or meadows. This was one of the reasons why, at mealtimes, men often remained seated and allowed themselves to be served by the women and girls, who were generally less exhausted by hard physical labour.[1]

I admit that I have painted a somewhat schematic picture here. My intention was largely, may I emphasize, to sound a warning note and to recommend the adoption of a broader and more comprehensive perspective.

10

Sunday Rest and 'the Demon Rest'

Anyone who imagines that, for a period lasting many centuries, Sunday rest meant a break from normal activities in order to restore the strength required for work would be guilty of a complete anachronism.

This is why this reference to rest needs to be examined through the eyes of a historian. In the first place, a distinction must be made between the rabbinical sabbath and Sunday rest. The former, backed up with the biblical references listed in chapter 1, and in particular those featuring in Leviticus and Numbers, celebrates God resting on the seventh day. Sunday rest, on the other hand, refers to the first day of creation, described in Genesis, when God created light, and therefore, in anticipation, the resurrection of Jesus Christ, and is celebrated on the first day of the week – in other words, on a Sunday.

In the eyes of Christians, the pause in activities which is referred to by the term 'Sunday rest' is a way of obtaining eternal rest in God, or, in other words, salvation. The day of the Lord is not a day for idleness which simply opens the door to temptation and therefore makes the devil's work all the easier. Marking a pause in all activities allows the faithful to sanctify – in the various ways we will now explore – time devoted to God.

As early as 321, Emperor Constantine had decreed laws imposing Sunday rest, with the exception of agricultural work. On this subject, Paul Veyne emphasizes that the seven-day rhythm was indeed present in the pagan world. Towards the end of the fourth century, chariot races and theatrical performances were forbidden so as to ensure that people could go and listen to the sermon. This law was not, however, widely respected. The Council of Laodicea (364–381), forbade Christians remaining idle on the sabbath and ordered them to work on that day. On the other hand, all activity should, where possible, cease on the day of the Lord (Sunday). Subsequently, a series of councils set out the list of activities which the faithful should not undertake: essentially, aside from work on the land, these included commercial activities, legal transactions and ... hunting. Added to these, from the sixth century onwards, came the obligation to take part in 'the oblation of bread and wine', which would later come to be called the mass.[1]

Much later, the Council of Trent, which took place between 1545 and 1563 as a reaction to the Reformation, set out in more detail the meaning and the practicalities of Sunday rest. It listed the services which Catholics were expected to attend on the Lord's Day. With reference to our subject here, rest was perceived as a period of time destined to allow the faithful to acquire the spiritual nourishment that would enable them to obtain salvation more easily by listening to sermons and homilies and reciting prayers. Rest, in this context, was the condition of possibility for access to eternal happiness and not simply a pause in activities. Moreover, the Council Fathers reiterated and emphasized that no servile work should be undertaken on that day. As well as the obligation to attend mass, they also recommended taking part in other services, particularly vespers.

Perfectly logically, the Council Fathers forbade entertainments, public dances and celebrations in taverns or inns on the Lord's Day. Sunday, according to the Council of Trent, also meant avoiding religious celebrations, and, in particular, marriage. In short, a ban was imposed on anything which might resemble idleness, apart from activities devoted to keeping Sundays holy. On this subject, Robert Beck cites Pierre Collet: '*The demon rest* is one of the most dangerous . . . and laziness only leads to impure thoughts.'[2] This is a notion which to some extent conflicts with, and even contradicts, the approach we have seen developed by Pascal, François de Sales and other seventeenth-century moralists, where the emphasis is on meditation and quietude and the rest in God which favours such a state.

Robert Beck adds that, according to the preaching of clerics faithful to the dictates of the Council, the need for rest was a sign of the state of imperfection which distinguishes man from Jesus – rest being confined, it should be emphasized, to life after death for those individuals who have successfully obtained their salvation and can enjoy it in divine peace. In a word, adds Beck, viewed from this perspective – and this is a key point – rest is not to be associated with what are considered earthly goods.

According to this same argument, there was, however, one form of rest which could indeed be celebrated, and that consisted in visiting graveyards, the resting places for deceased ancestors – an activity which emphasized the links between the living and the dead. Furthermore, when the entire time of Sunday rest was not completely taken up in attendance at religious services, the faithful could also devote themselves to pious reading or to charitable acts.

Until the middle of the eighteenth century, the meaning of Sundays and of Sunday rest remained largely unchallenged. So, for example, according to the bishop of Séez, in 240 parishes out of the 272 in his diocese, attendance at mass was at that time unanimously observed.[3] In the parish of Lonlay-l'Abbaye, where I spent my childhood, and which was part of this diocese, this was still the case during the years 1945–55. Better still, I recall an old country priest, who had come to preach in the parish during that period, assuring the farmers present that God would destroy their harvest if they continued to work on Sundays.

For the clergy, the greatest fear was that Sunday afternoons would end up being entirely given over to rest and that, as a result, they would be seen as a time for leisure and even for festive occasions. Indeed, from the pastors' perspective, the period of rest should ideally be filled with a variety of religious occupations. So it was that, in 1710, in the diocese of La Rochelle, the bishop decreed the following: 'Parish priests must help the faithful to fill the whole day with religious observance: morning prayer, the holy mass, the Sunday sermon, family instruction, vespers, catechism, evening prayer.'[4] The bishop forbade anything which might resemble free time or which might be seen as an opportunity for entertainment and idleness. It was the responsibility of the parish priest to prevent Sunday from being a time of rest in the way it is understood in the twenty-first century. In this context, the concept of Sunday best, or, in other words, the practice of putting on clothes which were as radically different as possible to those worn during the week, when a whole range of tasks were carried out, was highly symbolic. But, once again, this was a sign of a holy day on which work was set aside rather than one devoted to rest.

According to Robert Beck, the period from the middle of the eighteenth century – more precisely, the decade from 1730 to 1740 – saw the gradual decline in the model denoting Sunday as a holy day and of the rest associated with it. The first victim of this process was the service of vespers.

During the same period, the ban on carrying out servile tasks on a Sunday was being increasingly challenged, a process which was inevitably damaging to the practice of rest. In France, under the Revolution, the history of rest was severely shaken up. The introduction of the *decadi* (the last day of the ten-day week), intended to replace Sunday as the day of rest, brought with it the strict obligation to rest during this new day. In the immediate aftermath of the coup of 18 fructidor year V (4 September 1797), this was reiterated even more firmly. Napoleon Bonaparte, the first consul, initially imposed a very different policy. In the words of a terse comment made by Portalis, a jurist from whom the first consul sought advice: 'The people must work' – a principle which indicates the government's hostility to any notion of rest amongst the working population. With this in mind, the number of religious public holidays was drastically reduced to four.[5] Later, in 1807, the emperor introduced the free use of time on Sundays, abruptly bringing to an end any notion of imposed rest. This turbulent history of regulated rest would meet with sporadic resistance from parishioners, particularly in rural parishes.

At the same time, a very different factor gradually began to exert an influence on the history of rest, though in the absence of any regulation. Coinciding with the gradual secularization of Sundays, the declining support for the Tridentine Sunday rest and the slow increase in the number of festive activities taking place on a Sunday, and unconnected with any desire to sanctify time, a major change was taking shape within the bourgeoisie in this second half of the age of the Age of Enlightenment. Very different from the notion of contemplative rest and from the festive, recreational rest of the working classes, the desire for a private life was steadily gaining strength amongst the bourgeoisie. The increasing prevalence of relationships founded on love brought with it an emphasis on a new conception of family life centred on the physical presence of the parents, on their affection for the children and involvement in their upbringing. As a result, within this milieu, Sundays began to be approached in a new way, which had nothing to do with secularization. I shall return to this later, in the context of the mid-nineteenth century, when this 'family-centred' approach to Sundays reached a peak.

However, something else was also undermining support for the post-Tridentine Sunday. Workers were beginning to demand a day of rest and entertainment. It was in response to this request that the concept of Holy Monday was introduced at that point: a public holiday in the place of a Sunday, during which it was possible to satisfy the desire for celebrations and entertainments and which could be considered as a non-religious form of rest.

During the first half of the nineteenth century, the growing appeal of games, dances and drinking changed the holy nature of Sundays, much to the displeasure of the clerics, particularly in rural areas. Highly significant, in this context, was the endless battle waged by the curé d'Ars[6] against any form of Sunday entertainment coinciding with religious services in his little parish. The holy priest saw such activities as the work of the devil and, moreover, claimed to be personally tormented by him on a permanent basis.

In the middle of the nineteenth century, when France was experiencing a Catholic renaissance marked by a slowing in the decline of religious observance and symbolized by the success of Marian apparitions, religious practices became increasingly bourgeois and family orientated. So, for example, the end of mass was seen much more as a social occasion, and Sunday lunch was a time when the family could gather together, prior to the Sunday afternoon stroll. Put briefly, although Sunday rest was still observed, it began to be associated more with relaxation than with any religious connotation.

During the same period a certain specific form of boredom paradoxically started to be associated with Sunday afternoons within these bourgeois and artistic circles. This day of rest brought to a halt the 'urban machine' described by Maxime Du Camp in Paris at the time. Baudelaire was particularly sensitive to this Sunday boredom, as were, subsequently, a considerable number of other writers and artists of every genre. In the eyes of the impoverished student described by Jules Vallès, in 1860, Sunday was 'the colour of boredom, of despair and of emptiness'. On one such day, the character finds himself wondering 'where to kill time, where to slit the throat of boredom'.[7] For the migrant building worker who had come all the way from the Creuse, the absence of work on the Sunday, and the enforced rest that came with it, left him silently watching the River Seine flow past while dreaming about the region of his birth, which had now become an 'internalized country'.

No one else in the nineteenth century was as intensely affected by this Sunday boredom as the poet Georges Rodenbach. Let us listen to him, like the steady pulse behind this study, as he describes this dark mood almost in the form of a personal journal to which he devotes a considerable number of pages. I will confine myself to a few short extracts; first of all, he interweaves his dread of Sundays, with their inevitable rest and the accompanying boredom, with memories of his childhood:

> Sundays are always like those of childhood:
> An empty day, a sad day, a pale day, a bare day;
> a long day like a day of fasting and abstinence –
> of boredom[8] . . .

Or else:

> Sundays of times past, tedium of the dominical
> where the bells chimed as if for funerals,
> spreading over our souls a dread of death.[9]

As though harking back to the requiem and his constant yearnings for the past, Rodenbach sets out to describe in detail what rest felt like on this dreary day:

See how Sunday rest haunts me
And already seems to me a bitter rest,
The empty rest of a beach once the tide is out,
The dead beach of a long and endless Sunday
Congealing the distant silence of the sands.[10]

And Rodenbach embarks on a catalogue of all the things he hates:

Sunday: the sense of being in exile on that day,
A long day coloured by the sadness of the church bells,
And always this long Sunday keeps returning!
Ah, the sad bouquet of Sunday hours;
Like a sad bouquet of flowers slowly
Dying in a glass of water on a white cloth . . .
How can I escape it? How avoid it?
This day of half-mourning with faded colours
Where my idle heart drifts away in smoke,
I am obsessed with it, afraid of it, chilled by it.[11]

And returning to the funereal theme: 'The languor of a Sunday and its dreary boredom / Prevents us from savouring the exhilaration of living'; or: 'Sunday is the day where we hear the bells tolling! / Sunday is the day when our thoughts turn to death!'[12]

It would be too simplistic to say that the symbolist poet had completely lost sight of the religious significance of Sundays. Quite the contrary in fact, since, in his very frequent references to Sunday, we sense a reminder of death and a nostalgia for the holy requiem which was once associated with it. In this range of emotions associated with Sundays, rest is interwoven with boredom and brings his thoughts back to the requiem of long ago.

The sad tinge of Sunday evening rest serves as a leit-motif which extends into the twentieth century, where it finds its expression in film and songs. Emphasis is placed in particular, on this day of rest, on the boredom experienced by children and by individuals prone to sadness – a sentiment echoed in the songs of Charles Trenet and Juliette Greco.

11

Fatigue and Rest

My intention here is to not to focus on fatigue in itself[1] – and, even less, on exhaustion – but simply to examine the relationship between fatigue and rest within the context of a history of the latter. This relationship assumes a vital historical importance in the sense that, over the last two centuries, it has been instrumental in shaping the main definition of rest as a cure for fatigue.

We have seen that, over the course of time, this has by no means always been the case. For a long period, upheaval, anxiety and preoccupation were perceived as the enemies of a rest associated with quietude and with a peaceful existence, constantly threatened by boredom and idleness, regarded as the antechambers to the mortal sin of laziness.

In the nineteenth century, while the working population was feeling the effects of the Industrial Revolution, with its attendant reduction in rest time and increased levels of fatigue, the privileged and cultivated classes were discovering a form of rest which was closely linked to the considerable amount of time they now had at their disposal. This new type of rest reflected the growing interest in self-discovery rather than the need to restore the strength needed for physical work and involved an increased emphasis on personal time which, to some extent, echoed the aims and customs of the classical *otium*.

In the context of this study, what is significant about this conception of rest is that it represents a desire to abandon time as measured by the hands of the clock and instead take control of personal time 'in order to gain a greater sense of self through the body, the senses, the emotions, the imagination and the mind'. This led to a desire for rest, tranquillity, silence and escape, combined with a determination to avoid both idleness and boredom thanks to a radically new temporal framework, a revolution in how time could be used.

Amongst the bourgeoisie, this new approach to time gradually came to be regarded as a fundamental requirement. A considerable number of jobs and professions – and, even better, retirement itself – allowed individuals to exercise control over their own time thanks to a relative freedom in terms of professional commitments. The availability of time, and the potential for rest and leisure that came with it, began to be seen as a determining factor in social status. As a result, many individuals belonging to social elites found themselves experiencing what might be described as a gratified idleness, a conspicuous inactivity.

The risk inherent in this situation was that, within these circles, the resultant idleness, or rest as it came to be referred to, could lead to boredom, a cause of cerebral fatigue and resentment. This relative emptiness of time within certain social strata, referred to by Stendhal as early as in 1837 – and therefore well before Veblen – as 'the leisured class', makes its appearance in a history of rest no longer subject to industrial fatigue – a factor often overlooked.

For many individuals in this milieu, their professional status was largely a façade and did not involve anything very assiduous in terms of work. This meant that the amount of time at their disposal allowed them ample opportunity for rest, often devoted to cultural pursuits. Amongst these categories were lawyers with few cases, doctors without many patients, magistrates with ample leisure time, former soldiers, and 'industrialists' who had leased out their factories.

The nineteenth century, the era of the Industrial Revolution, corresponded to a period in which – at least in its early years – a considerable number of individuals from social elites, both large and small, found themselves living fulfilled and comfortable lives, enjoying the generous amount of time at their disposal and the corresponding opportunities for rest. In addition, there was also the temptation of a life of leisure, particularly appealing at that time, which combined availability, an unlimited amount of spare time and the choice of many different forms of rest, whether in the form of the leisurely walks described by Balzac with reference to individuals from these circles, and where the very act of walking meant that the person in question had time to himself, or those more infrequent walks organized by some local learned society. Not to mention, of course, the delights of poring over private collections or, more simply, the pleasures of conversation. And, for the wives of these individuals, their principal activity consisted in ostentatiously drawing attention to the amount of empty time they had at their disposal.

A number of writers have emphasized and sometimes glorified this sense of having time to spare, this temporal void, this passivity of the body and the mind, all of which, for Joseph Joubert, writing at the dawn of the century, represented the conditions for a possible rebirth of the self.

Until the middle of the nineteenth century, both in the city and in the countryside – and in the context of certain crafts this continued right up to the middle of the twentieth century – the distinction between fatigue and rest was a subtle one for workers. The scorn reserved for idleness, often regarded as shiftlessness (see chapter 9 above with reference to the countryside), which prevailed in these circles, and the value attributed to a task well executed, meant that any references to rest tended to be ignored. Nevertheless, even if 'doing nothing' was scarcely conceivable, rest was by no means absent. For the craftsman, as for the agricultural worker, as we have already seen, working time was not always filled to capacity and strictly timed but instead was punctuated by micro-breaks in activity. During working hours, the individual managed his own time, interspersing work with periods of rest. Working hours alternated with many short pauses which coincided with various different occasions: mealtimes, the siesta during harvest-time, travelling from one place to another, social encounters, 'drinking bouts'. Put briefly, short, fragmented intervals of rest found their way, though not in any systematic manner, into the very heart of the working day. Moreover, these periods of rest were rarely confined to single individuals.

The first Industrial Revolution, that of the steam engine, dramatically modified the history of rest, even though the traditional interspersing of brief intervals of non-work in the midst of working hours still persisted in many sectors. In the mechanized workshop and, even more, in the factory there was an increasing demand for accuracy and, as a result, time was strictly measured. The length of any breaks was tightly defined, and those brief moments of traditional rest which had been surreptitiously introduced into working time became a thing of the past. In these places, the freedom to take a short break was driven out by the constant rhythm of the machines, and, furthermore, any slowing of pace was no longer tolerated. New forms of fatigue began to manifest themselves, the result of the highly controlled working rhythm and of the disappearance of those little gaps which had previously made it possible to snatch brief periods of rest.

In Western countries, the 1870s onwards saw a heightened awareness of the negative effects of exhaustion, with all its attendant risks, the dangers associated with overworking, and with mental and intellectual exhaustion[2] and a growing demand for sufficient rest to stem the proliferation of these damaging physiological and psychological effects. This multifaceted movement resulted in an insistence on the provision of regular opportunities to regain strength and to preserve energy. As a result, a new physiological and psychological science of work began to develop.

The study of industrial fatigue meant that minimum times for sleep and leisure and – particularly relevant in the context of this study – rest were measured and recommended. The history of rest, whether collective or individual, was severely shaken up when people began to demand free time, calculated differently on an individual basis. All this new data tended to obliterate the rich historical depictions of rest. It was in this context that the European governments decided to introduce laws controlling the relationship between fatigue and rest, and in particular those imposing Sunday rest, or weekly rest as it was sometimes referred to, in a move to satisfy the anti-clerical movement.

Gradually, the calculation of time-frames became more precise. From the USA came the 'three eights' theory – in other words, the division of each 24-hour period into eight hours of sleep, eight hours of work and eight hours of rest or leisure.

This triggered a revolution in the history of rest. From that point on, instead of being able to use time freely, in a state of quietude or self-reflection, there was simply the legalized breakdown of time; consequently, this meant that everything that had previously contributed to the rich history of rest ended up being undermined. In this respect, fatigue, exhaustion and the resulting effects on mental states, etc., in a sense drained all interest and variety from the history of rest, reducing it to a plainer, more simplified version. And, incidentally, any attempts on the part of the faithful to maintain the holy character of rest, its grandeur, its capacity to develop personal energy and encourage self-reflection, proved to be in vain.

Nevertheless, at the same time, and as a consequence of the study of the physiology and psychology of fatigue, a heightened interest in the therapeutic value of rest was manifesting itself, and it is to this that I shall now turn my attention.

It was at this point that science – and this is crucial in the context of our goal here – set about studying, analysing and breaking down into its constituent parts a rest now very different from the one that had been understood and advocated for centuries.

Rest found itself elevated to the status of a natural need which was itemized and broken down. The mathematics of rest became an essential component serving a variety of goals. The resulting calculations listed the benefits of rest, a process of rebuilding, of calming and of revival. Rest provided protection from addiction, from problems then considered as social scourges – potentially leading to degeneration – in particular, the ravages of alcoholism and, above all, as we shall see in the next chapter, of tuberculosis. In this context, the notion of rest took on a hitherto unknown significance and dimension. The various elements of this period constitute what I am tempted to refer to as 'the great century of rest'. They became apparent at a time when, it is worth repeating, the former riches associated with rest were fading and even disappearing completely.

But there was more besides. Doctor Charles Féré, one of the leading lights on degeneration in this late nineteenth century, associated rest with the power to reduce the number of suicides, to lower crime levels and even . . . to encourage saving. All of which indicates a desire to attribute significant importance to rest within the context of a secularized morality and at the precise moment when its association with a holy existence was being largely undermined.

In conclusion to this chapter, it is clear that, in the late nineteenth century, rest had become one of the most fundamental components of our culture. It bound together notions of fatigue, of health and of well-being. It was part of the debate on social scourges. It haunted the anti-clericals. It insinuated itself into the moral code. All this at a time when the nature and status of rest was being subjected to the most intense scrutiny since the seventeenth century. And no mention has so far been made of another factor that underpins its importance: the synchroneity of rest reinforces social cohesion and contributes to a fulfilled family life.

And yet it is impossible to ignore the fact that, at this time, in the view of those who were particularly attentive to the benefits of work, rest, with the associated availability of time to yourself, could provoke, and even sharpen, an obsessional fear of loss.

12

Therapeutic Rest from the End of the Nineteenth to the Middle of the Twentieth Century

Previously, two different modes of rest were linked to health: one, it goes without saying, in which the need for rest was felt and prescribed during periods of convalescence, and the other, referred to earlier in this book, where rest was associated with invalids and those prone to melancholy. From the end of the nineteenth until the middle of the twentieth century, a new and specific type of rest came into being. This was the rest prescribed for patients afflicted by tuberculosis, one of the social scourges which inspired terror at that time.

From the mid-nineteenth century onwards, as Pierre Guillaume demonstrates in his powerful book on the history of this illness,[1] the conviction that tuberculosis was highly contagious gradually gained ground. Considerable energy was being devoted at that time to identify the transmission agent – Koch's bacillus, discovered in 1882 – and to find a cure for the disease, and the range of products ostensibly capable of combating the illness was, as we shall see, expanding rapidly. Nevertheless, rest was still considered to be the most effective remedy. Moreover, the need to isolate patients with tuberculosis was increasingly regarded as an essential public health measure; hence the establishment of what would, for a considerable period, be seen as the temple of rest – the sanatorium.

The intensity of the crusade waged against tuberculosis is difficult to comprehend today. During the 1940s, schoolchildren, and I was one of them, still took part in the door-to-door sales of 'anti-tuberculosis stamps'. This awareness-raising campaign exceeded in intensity the one then being waged against alcoholism. Furthermore, the risk of degeneracy continued for a long time to cast its shadow over this scenario.

The sanatorium, temple of rest, at the height of its glory, was to some extent the continuation of a long-established tradition extending from an enthusiasm for rest taken in the midst of nature and the fashion for the 'fresh-air cure' advocated at the end of the eighteenth century and preceding the advent of the vogue for sun-bathing. This latter came at the end of a period during which the sun was regarded with abhorrence, particularly amongst medical circles, long anxious to preserve patients from what was judged to be its extremely damaging effects.[2]

This new vision of the benefits of the sun meant that, initially at least, sanitoriums were built by the sea, in keeping with the ancient belief of the therapeutic power of the latter. But, very rapidly, mountain locations were preferred, and it was in these mountain settings that many of what we might call temples of rest began to appear. The high altitude, the quality of the surrounding air, the known advantages of exposure to the sun were thought to enhance the benefits of rest recommended to the patients who found themselves confined within such establishments.

In order to contain infection, particularly within families, a period of rest in a sanitorium was, for more than half a century, widely considered as likely to offer the greatest hope of recovery.

As stated earlier, my intention was to avoid referring to works of fiction (see above) as a source of evidence. Allow me, however, to make an exception here. Amongst the considerable number of books on the subject of sanitoriums or those using the sanitorium as their setting – and we are reminded of Thomas Mann's *The Magic Mountain* – Paul Gadenne's novel *Siloé* stands out in particular. Indeed, reading the book, it is clear that this is in part a genuinely autobiographical account based on personal experience. On two occasions, the author found himself confined in one of these institutions. In this novel, his comments on the sanitorium and the enforced rest which was imposed there are astonishingly true to life.

Striking, first of all, is the description of the setting for this period of quarantine, a place where rest reigned supreme. The single room, the neutrality of the décor, the stylized furniture, the prevailing silence, the absence of visitors other than that of the elderly and overbearing nurse, the enforced scrutiny of the daily schedule, all indicate a medicalized form of rest stricter than any previously experienced and one which induced a kind of terror in the new patient. In these institutions, Gadenne has one of the patients say: 'You live as a crowd, but you think alone.'[3]

For most of the patients, what is new is the view from the windows of a mountain landscape where, at certain times, the distant peaks are illuminated by the sun's rays. In this temple, rest takes on a particular texture: it is difficult to fully enjoy it for most of the day, given the fact that the lights remain on and there is always a variety of external noises made by invisible individuals.

During the long days, the key moment is the obligatory 'silent rest cure'. This means complete rest for all patients during the first two hours of the afternoon – in other words, in what staff refer to as the 'cure period'. During this period, Paul Gadenne experienced 'a conspiracy made up of all the silences, . . . emanating from these supine bodies',[4] until, abruptly, the bell rings to announce the end of the 'rest cure', the doors bang and there is the sound of people rushing up and down the staircases. Those two hours of complete rest, in silence, Paul Gadenne adds, were the moments where the illness 'was felt in all its inevitability'.[5]

Within the sanatorium, rest was regarded as the ultimate cure. Admittedly, there were others: gold salts, lime salts, tuberculin, creosote, seawater, irradiated mustard – a package destined above all for the treatment of the most serious, and even desperate, cases. According to the doctors, 'a good cure', or a 'proper cure', consisted in resting each afternoon either in bed or on a chaise longue, together with regular checks on weight during the morning weigh-ins. This was what was generally considered to be the best approach for the majority of tuberculosis patients.

When their health improved, patients were given permission to move to one of the smaller annexes situated behind the main building. From there, they could take walks in the adjoining meadow. Their confinement gradually became more relaxed until they could at last leave the sanatorium, a much anticipated day and an occasion for celebration.

The use of sanitoriums gradually declined from the mid-twentieth century onwards. After the Second World War, the availability of antibiotics – and initially the use of Rimifon – rendered the sanitorium obsolete. The change was, however, a slow one. Sanatoriums survived longer than anyone might have predicted. As well as prescribing antibiotics for patients with tuberculosis, doctors continued to recommend periods of rest which were considered essential for a complete cure.

Finally, it is worth noting that this remedy, for a long time successfully used in the fight against tuberculosis, was not advocated with anything like the same enthusiasm when it came to dealing with the threat of other 'social scourges'. The treatment of syphilis, whether in its extreme form of *tabes dorsalis* or in the case of the victims of so-called hereditary syphilis – an illness which was not in fact hereditary – or of alcoholics, even those suffering from regular bouts of *delirium tremens*, did not call for the intense rest imposed on victims of tuberculosis, and the theatre organized by Doctor Charcot at the Salpêtrière Asylum to demonstrate the treatment of women suffering from severe hysteria was not based on rest, even though some of the patients were bedridden.

Perhaps it is worth mentioning, in the context of nineteenth-century medicine, advice given to those suffering from impotence – and incidentally to their wives – which recommended a period of rest to be taken in the countryside.

Conclusion

At first sight, we in the Western hemisphere might think of rest as a concept which has remained unchanged since the Stoics of ancient times first defined its characteristics. Yet, as we now see, this is by no means the case. These traits have continued to evolve over the course of the centuries. At the height of Christianity, the focus was essentially on eternal rest. At that time, faithful Christians set their sights on salvation above all and on the *requiem aeternam* believed to go with it. No account was taken of any relationship between rest and fatigue. On this earth, quietude and rest in God continued to be the main theme reiterated by the mystics of the time. From the Middle Ages, the idea persisted that those who remained passive throughout their lives and made no attempt to cultivate their souls would find themselves threatened by sin and by *acedia*.

A reading of the sixteenth- and seventeenth-century moralists shows that the antonym of rest was not fatigue but the endless turmoil of daily life. Being at rest meant first of all escaping this agitation and, when life was approaching its end, contemplating and organizing a retirement synonymous with rest. As for those who worked the land, in the course of their various activities they followed the rhythms of nature. What can be described as Sunday rest – the legacy of biblical sabbaths, codified by the councils of the time, and in particular by the Council of Trent – primarily meant devoting a specific period of time totally to God.

In the eighteenth century, the appeal of the pastoral context became more refined as an increased focus on self-awareness enriched the experience of rest, still seen as a moment of meditation. As a result, an increased emphasis began to be placed on the therapeutic value of rest. All kinds of cures were associated with enforced rest. Yet rest was still seen not as a means of combating fatigue but, rather, as a remedy for illnesses – described in great detail – or as a means of restoring a general state of good health amongst convalescents or valetudinarians. And this included rest in natural surroundings as prescribed by Robert Burton in the seventeenth century for those suffering from melancholia.

At the same time, during the Renaissance, rest in nature was extolled by numerous writers referring back to ancient idylls ranging from Virgil's *Bucolics* to Petrarch's sonnets. And, later, Rousseau described the new forms of rest he had experienced in the course of his wanderings or in the reveries inspired by his solitary walks.

In the nineteenth century, fatigue and rest became ever more closely linked, though without any negative effect on the association already established between rest and treatment. Indeed, the opposite was true.

From that time onwards, rest became a necessity in the context of both schools and factories. It began to feature high on the list of what people demanded and expected. It became a political subject, and, in the West, a number of laws on the subject were brought into force.

During the twentieth century, the need for rest gradually changed shape, and psychological fatigue began to be the dominant factor. Today we scarcely refer any longer to rest but to moments of relaxation, with the result that fatigue tends to be replaced by an element of stress, a kind of malaise which takes the form of 'burnout', for example.

We leave these variations behind us when we turn our attention to the great century of rest culminating – and ending – at the end of the 1950s; the decade of sea, sex and sun, of the advent of paid leave, and the heyday of flirting, another key symbol of this period, bringing with it a gentler version of desire and of sexual relationships, first conceived on the decks of transatlantic liners and in coastal resorts at the end of the nineteenth century.

At that time, the amorous activities of young people had not yet reached the stormy heights of the 1960s onwards, and it was at that point that the great century of rest began to fade in other ways. All along the coast, the range of activities on offer continued to expand. The development of aquatic sports such as sailing began to undermine the notion of physical rest symbolized by passive sunbathing, and eventually various other activities helped to destroy the previous hegemony of forms of rest which had gradually become outdated.

Leisure replaces rest. It fills up time. It takes up space.

Slowly, a distant legacy of the types of rest destined to combat – successively – melancholy, depression, neurasthenia and physical exhaustion, new forms of therapeutic rest began to appear. These were designed

Conclusion

to ease a whole range of problems, including those classified under the term of 'burn-out', still awaiting its ultimate social definition. But all this goes beyond the role of the historian, which is to understand the past and to avoid anachronisms.

Is the simple longing for rest in the midst of nature therefore in any way diminished by the omnipresence of the science and techniques relating to rest? Clearly this is by no means the case. As a grand finale to these variations, let us turn to the fascinating experience described by Francis Ponge during the final years of his life, when he was focusing his attention on what he called 'The Making of the Pre' – simply because, according to him, this green space was the ultimate place of rest, one that suggests 'a lying down'. On this 'vegetal-beach, fresh, supple, fertile', symbol of spring regrowth, everything appears 'united, simple, even, continual' and above all 'restful'. The pre 'stretched horizontally beneath our eyes for our relaxation' is the meadow of 'our repose', 'a place of eternal leisure'.[1] The place where this study comes to a halt, like the final full-stop marking the end of a book.

Notes

Chapter 1 Sabbath and Heavenly Rest

1 See the entry on 'Rest' in Jean Chevalier and Alain Gheerbrant, *A Dictionary of Symbols*. London: Penguin, 1996, pp. 797–8.

2 *The Jerusalem Bible*. London: Darton, Longman & Todd, 1966, Exodus 31, verses 12–14, p. 118.

3 Ibid., Exodus 31, verse 14, p. 118.

4 Ibid., Exodus 20, verses 8–10, p. 102.

5 Ibid., Exodus 34, verse 21, p. 122.

6 Ibid., Exodus 31, verse 15, p. 118.

7 Ibid., Exodus 35, verse 3, p. 123.

8 Ibid., Leviticus 23, verse 3, p. 159.

9 This citation is from the commentary to the French version of the Jerusalem Bible, cited by the author: *Bible de Jérusalem*. Paris: Editions du Cerf, 2001, p. 233.

10 *The Jerusalem Bible*, Leviticus 25, verses 3–6, p. 162.

11 John Milton, *Paradise Lost*, Book IV, 3.25. New York: W. W. Norton, 2005, p. 87.

---

12 Ibid., Book IV, 3.30, p. 87.
13 Ibid., Book IV, 6.10, p. 94.
14 Ibid., Book XII, 6.45, p. 303.

Chapter 2 Eternal Rest

1 Philippe Ariès, *Western Attitudes towards Death: From the Middle Ages to the Present*. Baltimore: Johns Hopkins University Press, 1979.

Chapter 3 Rest and Quietude

1 Blaise Pascal, *Pensées*. London: Penguin, 1995, p. 208.
2 Ibid.
3 Ibid.
4 Ibid., p. 40.
5 Acedia, which, for example, afflicted a number of monks in the Middle Ages, is a psychological illness condemned by the Church, since it was seen as a threat to faith and to hope.
6 Pascal, *Œuvres complètes*. Paris: Gallimard, 1954.
7 Pascal, *Pensées*, p. 41.
8 Ibid., p. 37.
9 Ibid., p. 40.
10 Pascal, *Œuvres complètes*, p. 1171.
11 Teresa d'Avila, *The Book of My Life*. Boston: New Seeds, 2007, pp. 104–6.
12 François de Sales, *Of the Love of God*. London: Rivingtons, 1888, p. 196. In the Bible, the Sulamite or Shuamite bride is the 'dearly beloved' in the Song of Songs.
13 Ibid.
14 Ibid., p. 197.
15 Ibid.

16 Ibid., p. 198.

17 Ibid., p. 199.

18 Ibid., p. 200.

19 Ibid.

20 Ibid., p. 201.

21 Jacques-Bénigne Bossuet, *Œuvres*. Paris: Gallimard, 1961. 'Sermon sur la mort', pp. 1084–5. English version 'Bossuet on Death' may be found at https://maelurain.wordpress.com/2015/03/28/bossuet-on-death/.

22 D. Mahony (ed.), *Panegyrics of The Saints: From the French of Bossuet and Bourdaloue*. London: Kegan Paul, Trench, Trubner & Co., 1924, p. 80.

23 Ibid., p. 82.

24 Jean Deprun, *La Philosophie de l'inquiétude en France au XVIII siècle*. Paris: Vrin, 1979.

Chapter 4 Retreat and Retirement in the Seventeenth and Eighteenth Centuries

1 Michel de Montaigne, *The Essays: A Selection*. London: Penguin, 2004, pp. 101, 102.

2 Ibid., p. 101.

3 Ibid., p. 102.

4 Ibid., p. 155.

5 Ibid., p. 156.

6 Ibid., p. 105.

7 Ibid., p. 107.

8 Ibid., p. 105.

9 Ibid., p. 101.

10 Ibid., p. 105.

11 Ibid., p. 106.

12 Ibid., pp. 103–4.

13 Ibid., p. 104.
14 La Rochefoucauld, *Collected Maxims and Other Reflections*. Oxford: Oxford University Press, 2007, p. 263.
15 Ibid.
16 Lucretius, *On the Nature of Things*. Indianopolis: Hackett, 2001, p. 93.
17 La Rochefoucauld, *Collected Maxims and Other Reflections*, p. 169.
18 Ibid., p. 171. The author cites J. Lafond, *Moralistes du XVII siècle*. Paris, Robert Laffont, 1992, p. 247.
19 Lafond, p. 278.
20 Ibid., p. 806.
21 Jean de La Bruyère, *'The Characters' of Jean de La Bruyère*. London: Routledge, 1929, p. 210.
22 Ibid., p. 285.
23 Ibid., p. 364.
24 Charles Rivière Dufresny, *Amusements sérieux et comiques*. Paris: Éditions Bossard, 1921, p. 66.
25 Denis Diderot, *Diderot's Thoughts on Art and Style: With Some of his Shorter Essays*, trans. Beatrix L. Tollemache. London: Remington, 1893, p. 242.
26 Denis Diderot, *Salons*, Vol. 1: *Salons de 1761 et 1765: Essai sur la peinture*. Paris: Brière, 1821, p. 465.
27 Joseph Joubert, *Carnets*. Paris: Gallimard, 1994, Vol. 1, p. 152.
28 Ibid., Vol. I, p. 621.
29 Ibid., Vol. II, p. 393.
30 Ibid., Vol. II, p. 444.
31 Ibid., Vol. II, p. 476.

Interlude

1 With the exception of his title of emperor, which was elective and could be not be passed on according to his wishes. In this Interlude, I refer to a number of publications on the life of Charles V, and in particular the admirable study by Pierre Chenu and Michèle Escamilla: *Charles Quint*. Paris: Fayard, 2000; also Paris: Tallandier, 2013 and 2020.

Chapter 5 Disgrace, an Opportunity for Rest

1 Alain Corbin 'Paris-province', in Pierre Nora (ed.), *Les Lieux de mémoire*. Paris: Gallimard, 1992, Part III: *Les France*, vol. 1: *Conflits et partages*, pp. 777–823.

2 Blaise Pascal, *Pensées*. London: Penguin, 1995, p. 41.

3 I have selected a source from Bussy-Rabutin's extensive body of personal writing. Madame de Sévigné, *Correspondance*. Paris: Gallimard, Vol. II, 1974.

4 Ibid., p. 1045.

5 Ibid., p. 1062.

6 Ibid., p. 1070.

7 Ibid., p. 986. The 'directors' here are of course 'spiritual directors' or confessors.

Chapter 6 Rest in the Midst of Confinement

1 Silvio Pellico (1789–1854) was an Italian patriot and writer who was imprisoned for ten years in Venice and Spielberg. Prince Louis-Napoléon Bonaparte (the future Napoléon III) spent six years in the Fortress of Ham before escaping in 1846.

2 Ivan Gontcharov, *Oblomov*. London: Penguin, 2005.

3 A reference to Molière's play *Les Fâcheux* (1661), translated into English as 'The Bores'.

4 Michel de Montaigne, *The Essays*. London: Penguin, 1993, p. 157.

5 Marguerite de Navarre, *The Heptameron*. London: Penguin, 2004, p. 10.

6 Ibid., pp. 66–70.

7 Xavier de Maistre, *Voyage Around My Room: Selected works of Xavier de Maistre*. New York: New Directions, 1994.

8 Xavier de Maistre, *Voyage autour de ma chambre*, ed. Florence Lotterie. Paris: Flammarion, 2003, p. 18.

9 Xavier de Maistre, *Voyage Around My Room*, p. 4.

10 *Diderot's Thoughts on Art and Style: With Some of His Shorter Essays*, ed. and trans. Beatriz L. Tollemache. London: Remington, 1893, p. 236.

11 Xavier de Maistre, *Voyage Around My Room*, pp. 9, 21.

12 Ibid., p. 32.

13 Ibid., pp. 78, 51.

Chapter 7 The Quest for Comfort

1 Jean de la Bruyère, *The 'Characters' of Jean de la Bruyère*. New York: Scribner & Welford, 1885, p. 428.

2 Georges Vigarello, 'Le fauteuil', in Pierre Singaravélou and Sylvain Venayre, *Histoire du monde en XIX siècle*. Paris: Pluriel, 2019, pp. 644ff. I have drawn closely on this article here.

3 Ibid., p. 645.

4 Ibid., p. 647.

5 Ibid.

6 On this subject, see the splendid article by Sébastien Roseaux, 'Le hamac', in Pierre Singaravélou and Sylvain Venayre, *Le Magasin du monde*. Paris: Fayard, 2020, pp. 385–9.

7 Xavier de Maistre, *Voyage Around My Room: Selected works of Xavier de Maistre*. New York: New Directions, 1994, pp. 16–17, 29.

Chapter 8 *Prelude*

1 Virgile, *Bucoliques, Georgiques*, Paris: Gallimard, 1997, preface by Florent Dupont, pp. 69, 89, and 105; and Paul Valéry, *Oeuvres*, Vol. 1. Paris: Gallimard, 1957. 'Variations sur le *Bucoliques*', pp. 207 and translation of *Bucoliques*, pp. 207–23.

2 Virgil, *The Ecologues and Georgics of Virgil*. London: Dent, 1907, pp. 30–46.

3 Martial, *Epigrams*, Book V. Oxford: Oxford World Classics, p. 93.

4 I explored this point in more detail in Alain Corbin, 'Les historiens et la fiction: usages, tentation, nécessité . . .', *Le Débat, histoire, politique, société*, no. 165, May–August 2011, pp. 57–61.

5 Ronsard, *Œuvres complètes*. Paris: Gallimard, Vol. 1, 1993; Vol. 2, 1994. Unless otherwise stated, English translations of the Ronsard poems cited here are by Helen Morrison.

6 Ibid., Vol. 1, p. 902.

7 This translation was found at www.hyperion-records.co.uk/tw.asp?w=W14722&t=GBLLH1332313&al=W14722_120323.

8 Ronsard, *Œuvres complètes*, Vol. 2, p. 951.

9 Ibid., Vol. 2, p. 351.

10 Ibid., Vol. 1, p. 785.

11 Ibid., Vol. 2, p. 416.

12 Ibid., Vol 2, p. 325.

13 Ibid., Vol. 1, p. 755. This translation found in Pierre de Ronsard, *Selected Poems*. London: Penguin, 2002, p. 30.

14 Ronsard, *Œuvres complètes*, Vol. 1, p. 703.

15 Ibid., Vol. 1, p. 705.

16 Ibid., Vol. 2, p. 692.

17 Ibid., Vol. 1, p. 706, p. 533.

18 *L'Astrée* is a pastoral novel published between 1607 and 1627 by Honoré d'Urfé. *Artamène ou le Grand Cyrus (Artamenes, or The Grand Cyrus)* is a novel by Madeleine de Scudéry which was published in ten episodes between 1649 and 1653.

19 Jean-Jacques Rousseau, *Reveries of a Solitary Walker*. Indianapolis: Hackett, 1992.

20 Ibid., p. 69.

21 Ibid., pp. 69–70.

22 Ibid., p. 70.

23 Ibid., p. 66.

24 Ibid., p. 67.

25 Ibid., p. 68.

26 Ibid., p. 103.

27 The French philosopher Emile-Auguste Chartier (1868–1951), known as Alain.

28 This citation, and all the following, are extracts from the entry on 'Repos', in Bescherelle, *Dictionnaire universel de la langue française*. Paris: Garnier frères, 1861.

29 This translation found in Thomas Carlyle, *The French Revolution: A History*. London: Chapman & Hall, 1885, p. 185.

30 Cf. John Byng Torrington (5th Viscount), *The*

Torrington Diaries. London: Eyre & Spottiswoode, 1954, pp. 87–108; and Alain Corbin, *Le Territoire du vide: l'Occident et le désir du rivage.* Paris: Aubier, 1988.

Chapter 9 A Rest for the Land

1 This phenomenon was one I observed and described in my book *Archaïsme et modernité en Limousin au XIX siècle, 1845–1880.* Paris: Rivière, 1975; repr. Limoges: Presses universitaires de Limoges, 2000.

Chapter 10 Sunday Rest and 'the Demon Rest'

1 For further information on these points, see Robert Beck's wonderful work *Histoire du dimanche de 1700 à nos jours.* Paris: Éditions de l'Atelier/Éditions Ouvrières, 1997. I have drawn on this book extensively here. On the subject of Emperor Constantine, see Paul Veyne, 'Quand le monde est devenu chrétien', in Veyne, *Une insolite curiosité.* Paris: Robert Laffont, 2020 – in particular 'Toujours le dimanche', pp. 806–8.

2 Pierre Collet, quoted by Robert Beck in *Histoire du dimanche*, p. 61.

3 Ibid., p. 35.

4 Ibid., p. 61.

5 In Alain Corbin, *Village Bells: Sound and Meaning in the 19th-Century French Countryside.* New York: Columbia University Press, p. 119.

6 The *curé d'Ars* is a reference to the French parish priest John Vianney (1786–1859), who was well known for his work in the parish of Ars.

7 Cited in Julia Csergo, 'Extension et mutation du

loisir citadin', in Alain Corbin (ed.), *L'Avènement des loisirs*. Paris: Aubier, 1995, p. 131.

8 Georges Rodenbach, *Œuvre poétique*. Paris: Mercure de France, 2008, Vol. 1, p. 240; Eng. trans. in Rodenbach, *Poems*. Todmorden: Arc, 2017, p. 65. Other poems translated here by Helen Morrison.

9 Rodenbach, *Œuvre poétique*, Vol. 1, p. 241; Eng. trans. in *Poems*, p. 65.

10 Rodenbach, *Œuvre poétique* Vol. 1, p. 240.

11 Ibid., pp. 239–40.

12 Ibid.

Chapter 11 Fatigue and Rest

1 On the subject of fatigue, I refer here to Georges Vigarello's brilliant book *A History of Fatigue: From the Middle Ages to the Present*. Cambridge: Polity, 2022. On a more modest note, with reference to rest, I also refer here to Alain Corbin, *L'Avènement des loisirs*. Paris: Aubier, 1995, and specifically to the chapter entitled 'La fatigue, le repos et la conquête du temps', pp. 276–98.

2 See Vigarello, *A History of Fatigue*, chapter 23, 'The World of "Mental Fatigue"'.

Chapter 12 Therapeutic Rest from the End of the Nineteenth to the Middle of the Twentieth Century

1 Pierre Guillaume, *Du désespoir au salut: les tuberculeux aux XIX et XX siècles*. Paris: Aubier, 1986.

2 See Christophe Grangery, 'Le soleil, ou la saveur des temps insoucieux', in Alain Corbin (ed.), *La Pluie*,

le soleil et le vent: une histoire de la sensibilité au temps qu'il fait. Paris: Aubier, 2013, pp. 37–68.
3 Paul Gadenne, *Siloé.* Paris: Éditions du Seuil, 1974, p. 110.
4 Ibid., p. 135.
5 Ibid., p. 134.

Conclusion
1 Francis Ponge, *The Making of the Pré*, trans. Lee Fahnestock. Columbia: University of Missouri Press, 1979, pp. 25, 57, 119, 179, 115.

Index

Index

Index

Index

Index